CYBERSECURITY & DATA INNOVATION FOR BUSINESS TRANSFORMATION

Nnamdi Rex Onwubuche

Published by: Prodigy Press

Table of contents

Preface

Cybersecurity has moved from the background of organizational operations to the very center of how modern enterprises function, compete, and survive. What was once viewed as a technical concern handled quietly by information technology teams is now a defining factor in business credibility, financial stability, and long term growth. Every transaction processed, every decision automated, and every insight generated through data relies on systems that must be protected, trusted, and resilient.

This book was written to address that shift.

Digital transformation has changed the way organizations create value. Cloud platforms, intelligent automation, advanced analytics, and interconnected systems have enabled speed, scale, and efficiency that were unimaginable only a few years ago. At the same time, these advances have introduced new forms of risk. Cyber threats are no longer opportunistic or random. They are deliberate, adaptive, and often financially or strategically motivated. Attackers study business processes, exploit operational dependencies, and target data as an asset with measurable value.

In parallel, expectations around governance and accountability have increased. Regulators demand stronger controls. Customers expect privacy and reliability. Investors look closely at how organizations manage digital risk. In this environment, cybersecurity can no longer be treated as a standalone function. It must be understood as an integral part of business strategy, financial management, and operational design.

Cybersecurity and Data Innovation for Business Transformation was developed with this reality in mind. The purpose of this book is not to overwhelm readers with technical specifications or isolated security tools.

Instead, it aims to provide a structured way of thinking about cybersecurity as a system of decisions, controls, and data driven insights that support business objectives. Security is most effective when it enables informed action, reduces uncertainty, and strengthens confidence across the organization.

One of the central ideas explored throughout this book is the role of data in shaping cybersecurity outcomes. Modern security environments generate vast amounts of information. Logs, alerts, transaction records, behavioral signals, and system metrics all provide clues about risk and performance. However, data alone does not create security. Without proper context, governance, and analytical discipline, information becomes noise. This book emphasizes how data innovation can be harnessed to improve threat detection, prioritize response, and support strategic decision making.

Artificial intelligence and automation play a significant role in this discussion. As systems grow more complex, manual security processes struggle to keep pace. Automation can reduce response time, improve consistency, and free professionals to focus on higher level analysis. Yet automation also introduces new considerations around trust, oversight, and accountability. This book approaches AI powered cybersecurity with balance, highlighting both its potential and its limitations, and stressing the importance of human judgment in guiding intelligent systems.

Another key theme is the intersection of cybersecurity with risk management and compliance. Many organizations approach compliance as an external obligation rather than an internal discipline. Checklists are completed, audits are passed, and controls are documented, but underlying risks remain poorly understood. This book encourages a deeper view of compliance, one that connects regulatory requirements with actual operational risk and financial exposure. By aligning security controls with governance frameworks and business priorities, organizations can move beyond compliance as a minimum requirement toward resilience as a strategic goal.

Financial analytics is also given significant attention in this work. Cybersecurity decisions often involve trade offs. Investments in controls, monitoring, and response capabilities must be justified against cost, impact, and opportunity. Yet many organizations lack clear methods for measuring the financial implications of cyber risk. This book introduces financial models and performance tracking approaches that help translate security efforts into terms that executives, boards, and financial stakeholders can understand. When cybersecurity is linked to measurable outcomes, it gains clarity, credibility, and sustained support.

Frameworks and standards are important, but they must be adapted to the realities of each organization. Constraints such as budget, talent availability, legacy systems, and organizational culture shape how security strategies are implemented. This book acknowledges those constraints and focuses on practical approaches that improve decision making and cost efficiency rather than theoretical perfection.

Integration is another recurring concept. Cybersecurity does not exist in isolation from finance, operations, or leadership. When security teams operate separately from business units, blind spots emerge. When data is fragmented across systems, risk becomes difficult to assess. This book argues for an integrated approach in which cybersecurity, data analytics, and business transformation move together. Such alignment improves visibility, strengthens accountability, and reduces the likelihood of unexpected failures.

The intended audience for this book reflects the broad scope of these challenges. Cybersecurity professionals will find discussions that connect technical controls with governance, analytics, and business impact. Business leaders will gain a clearer understanding of how security decisions influence performance, reputation, and strategic flexibility. Graduate students will encounter concepts that bridge academic theory with operational practice. Financial technology professionals will see how cybersecurity, analytics, and financial systems converge in digitally driven enterprises.

This work is also motivated by the growing gap between awareness and action. Many organizations understand that cybersecurity is important, yet struggle to translate that understanding into effective systems and behaviors. Policies exist, but they are not followed. Tools are deployed, but insights are not acted upon. This book seeks to close that gap by emphasizing clarity, discipline, and continuous improvement. Cybersecurity is treated as an evolving practice rather than a static achievement.

The timing of this book, with an expected release in November 2021, reflects a period of heightened digital reliance. Global disruptions accelerated remote work, cloud adoption, and digital service delivery. At the same time, cyber incidents increased in scale and impact, exposing weaknesses in existing defenses. While circumstances continue to evolve, the lessons from this period remain relevant. Organizations must design security strategies that can adapt to uncertainty and change.

Readers are encouraged to approach this book as a guide rather than a prescription. No single model fits every organization. The value lies in understanding principles, asking better questions, and making informed choices. Cybersecurity, when grounded in data and aligned with strategy, becomes a source of strength rather than a constraint.

Ultimately, this book is about confidence. Confidence that digital systems can be relied upon. Confidence that risks are visible and managed. Confidence that decisions are supported by accurate, timely information. When organizations achieve that confidence, they are better positioned to innovate, compete, and grow in an increasingly connected world.

Foreword

Cybersecurity has become one of the defining challenges of our time, not because technology has failed, but because success has made systems more valuable, more connected, and more exposed. As organizations digitize operations, automate decisions, and rely on data as a strategic asset, the consequences of insecurity extend far beyond technical disruption. They affect trust, financial stability, regulatory confidence, and long term competitiveness.

This book arrives at an important moment.

For many years, cybersecurity conversations were dominated by tools, controls, and incident response. Those elements still matter, but they are no longer sufficient. Modern enterprises require a deeper understanding of how security interacts with data, analytics, governance, and business performance. Cyber risk today is not only a technical risk. It is a business risk, a financial risk, and a leadership challenge.

Cybersecurity and Data Innovation for Business Transformation addresses this reality with clarity and discipline. It does not treat cybersecurity as an isolated function or a compliance exercise. Instead, it presents security as an integrated system of decisions, informed by data and shaped by organizational priorities. This perspective is increasingly necessary in a world where digital systems underpin nearly every aspect of economic and social activity.

One of the strengths of this work is its balanced approach. The book does not overstate the promise of technology, nor does it underestimate the complexity of implementation. Artificial intelligence, automation, and advanced analytics are discussed as powerful tools, but always within the context of governance, accountability, and human judgment. This balance is essential. Organizations that rely solely on technology without strategy often find themselves reacting to risk rather than managing it.

The emphasis on data driven insight is particularly valuable. Security teams generate enormous volumes of information, yet many organizations struggle to convert that information into action. By framing cybersecurity as a data problem as much as a technical one, this book highlights how analytics can improve visibility, prioritization, and decision making. When leaders understand what their data is telling them, they are better equipped to allocate resources, manage trade offs, and respond effectively under pressure.

Another important contribution of this book lies in its treatment of risk and compliance. Too often, compliance is viewed as a box to be checked, disconnected from operational reality. This work challenges that mindset by linking regulatory requirements to actual risk exposure and business outcomes. It encourages readers to think critically about why controls exist, how they should function, and how they can be measured for effectiveness. This approach supports resilience rather than minimal adherence.

The integration of financial analytics into cybersecurity discussions is also timely. Security investments compete with other strategic priorities, and leaders are increasingly asked to justify spending in clear and measurable terms. By introducing financial models and performance tracking concepts, this book helps bridge the gap between technical necessity and executive understanding. It provides a language for discussing security in terms of value, cost efficiency, and long term return.

Equally important is the focus on real world application. The ideas presented here are grounded in practical considerations such as organizational constraints, legacy systems, and human behavior. This realism makes the book relevant not only to seasoned professionals, but also to emerging leaders and graduate students who are preparing to work in complex environments. The ability to connect theory with practice is one of the hallmarks of effective professional guidance.

The audience for this book is intentionally broad. Cybersecurity professionals will find perspectives that extend beyond tools into governance and strategy. Business leaders will gain insight into how security decisions shape performance and risk posture. Financial technology practitioners will see how data, security, and analytics converge in modern enterprises. Students and researchers will encounter a framework that connects academic concepts with operational relevance.

The period leading up to the expected release of this book in November 2021 underscored the urgency of its themes. Rapid shifts to remote work, accelerated digital adoption, and a rise in cyber incidents exposed both strengths and weaknesses in organizational defenses. Those conditions forced many leaders to confront gaps in visibility, preparedness, and decision making. While circumstances continue to evolve, the lessons remain applicable. Resilient organizations are those that treat cybersecurity as a continuous, data informed discipline rather than a one time project.

What sets this book apart is its insistence on integration. Cybersecurity is not presented as a barrier to innovation, but as an enabler of sustainable transformation. When security strategies are aligned with business objectives and supported by reliable data, organizations gain confidence to innovate responsibly. That confidence is essential in a competitive and uncertain digital landscape.

As someone who has observed the evolution of cybersecurity across industries, I believe this work makes a meaningful contribution to the field. It encourages readers to think critically, act deliberately, and view security as a shared responsibility rather than a siloed function. It reinforces the idea that effective cybersecurity is built through informed leadership, disciplined execution, and continuous learning.

I commend this book to anyone seeking to understand how cybersecurity and data innovation can support lasting business transformation. The insights offered here will be valuable not only for addressing current challenges, but also for preparing for those yet to come.

Introduction

The digital age has reshaped how organizations think, operate, and compete. Information now moves faster than ever before, decisions are increasingly automated, and value is created as much through data as through physical assets. From financial services and healthcare to manufacturing and public infrastructure, digital systems have become the backbone of modern enterprise. Yet as reliance on technology has grown, so too has vulnerability. Cybersecurity is no longer a background concern. It is a defining condition for stability, growth, and trust.

For many organizations, this shift has been uncomfortable.

Cybersecurity was historically framed as a technical function, managed by specialists and discussed only when something went wrong. Security teams focused on perimeter defenses, access controls, and incident response, while business leaders concentrated on growth, efficiency, and innovation. That separation is no longer sustainable. Today, cyber incidents can halt operations, distort financial reporting, trigger regulatory action, and permanently damage reputation. In a data driven economy, the security of digital systems is inseparable from business performance.

This book begins from the understanding that cybersecurity has become a strategic discipline. It influences how organizations design processes, manage risk, allocate resources, and make decisions. More importantly, it determines whether digital transformation delivers long term value or introduces fragile complexity.

Cybersecurity and Data Innovation for Business Transformation is written to help bridge the gap between technical security practices and business realities. It recognizes that organizations do not operate in controlled laboratory environments. They function under pressure, with limited budgets, competing priorities, legacy systems, and human constraints. In such conditions, effective cybersecurity is not about eliminating risk entirely. It is about understanding risk, prioritizing action, and building systems that remain dependable even when challenged.

A defining characteristic of the modern cyber landscape is interconnectedness. Systems rarely stand alone. Applications depend on shared infrastructure. Data flows across platforms, vendors, and geographic boundaries. Decisions made in one system influence outcomes in another. This interconnectedness amplifies both opportunity and risk. A single vulnerability can propagate across operations, while a single insight can improve performance at scale. Cybersecurity strategies must therefore account for relationships between systems, data, and decisions.

Threats have evolved alongside this complexity. Cyber adversaries are no longer limited to exploiting software flaws. They target business processes, human behavior, and governance weaknesses. Attacks are often designed to manipulate outcomes rather than simply disrupt systems. Fraud schemes exploit analytics gaps. Ransomware targets operational dependencies. Data breaches undermine trust and regulatory standing. Understanding these threats requires more than technical expertise. It requires insight into how organizations function and where they are most exposed.

Data plays a central role in addressing these challenges. Every digital interaction leaves a trace. Logs, transaction records, behavioral patterns, and performance metrics provide signals about system health and risk. However, the presence of data does not guarantee insight. Many organizations collect vast amounts of information but lack the structures to analyze it meaningfully. Alerts are generated faster than they can be interpreted. Reports are produced without influencing decisions. This book argues that cybersecurity must be grounded in disciplined data practices that turn information into actionable intelligence.

Artificial intelligence and automation are increasingly presented as solutions to the scale and speed of modern cyber threats. When applied effectively, they can enhance detection, reduce response time, and support consistency in security operations. When applied carelessly, they can obscure accountability and introduce new forms of risk. This book approaches intelligent security technologies with realism. It examines how automation can strengthen defenses while emphasizing the need for governance, transparency, and human oversight.

Risk management and compliance are also reframed throughout this work. Too often, compliance is treated as a static obligation disconnected from operational risk. Controls are implemented to satisfy audits rather than to protect value. This approach creates a false sense of security. Cybersecurity must be evaluated in terms of how well it reduces exposure, supports resilience, and aligns with organizational objectives. By linking risk frameworks with data driven assessment and governance structures, organizations can move beyond superficial compliance toward meaningful control.

Financial considerations are another critical but frequently overlooked dimension of cybersecurity. Security initiatives require investment, yet many organizations struggle to articulate their financial value. Decisions are made based on fear, anecdote, or regulatory pressure rather than informed analysis. This book introduces financial analytics as a lens through which cybersecurity can be evaluated and governed. Cost efficiency, return on security investment, and performance measurement are explored as tools for aligning security decisions with business strategy.

The structure of this book reflects the layered nature of these issues. Early chapters establish the business context of cybersecurity and outline foundational principles. Subsequent chapters examine evolving threats, data driven intelligence, and AI powered automation. Governance, compliance, and financial analytics are then integrated into the discussion, highlighting how security decisions influence organizational outcomes. Later chapters focus on real world application, showing how these concepts shape decision making, cost control, and operational resilience.

The audience for this book is intentionally diverse. Cybersecurity professionals will find discussions that connect technical controls with analytics and governance. Business leaders will gain clarity on how security affects financial performance, risk posture, and strategic flexibility. Graduate students will encounter a framework that links academic concepts with practical realities. Financial technology professionals will see how cybersecurity, data innovation, and financial systems intersect in digitally transformed enterprises.

The expected release of this book in November 2021 reflects a period of accelerated digital reliance. Global events pushed organizations toward remote work, cloud services, and automation at unprecedented speed. At the same time, cyber incidents increased in frequency and impact, exposing weaknesses in visibility, preparedness, and decision making. While technology continues to evolve, the lessons from this period remain instructive. Organizations that succeed are those that treat cybersecurity as a continuous, data informed practice rather than a one time project.

At its core, this book is about enabling confidence in digital systems. Confidence that data can be trusted. Confidence that risks are visible and managed. Confidence that innovation can proceed without undermining stability. When cybersecurity is integrated with data innovation and business strategy, it becomes not a constraint, but a foundation for sustainable growth.

Chapter 1

Cybersecurity as a Business Imperative

Cybersecurity has steadily moved from the periphery of organizational concerns to the core of how modern enterprises function. In earlier decades, security was largely perceived as a technical requirement, addressed after systems were deployed and often considered successful if incidents were rare or quickly resolved. Today, that view no longer holds. Digital systems now support essential business operations, financial transactions, strategic planning, and customer engagement. As a result, cybersecurity has become inseparable from business continuity, performance, and credibility.

At its core, a business exists to create value. In a digital economy, much of that value is generated, stored, and exchanged through information systems. Customer data, financial records, analytics models, intellectual property, and operational processes all depend on the reliability of digital infrastructure. When these systems are compromised, the impact extends beyond technical disruption. It affects revenue, regulatory standing, decision quality, and public trust. Cybersecurity therefore must be understood not as a defensive add on, but as a foundational element of business strategy.

One of the primary drivers of this shift is the changing nature of risk. Traditional business risks such as market volatility, supply chain disruption, and operational failure remain important, but cyber risk now intersects with each of them. A single cyber incident can disrupt supply chains, halt production, distort financial data, and expose organizations to legal action. In many cases, the financial impact of such incidents exceeds that of more familiar risks. This reality has forced executives and boards to reconsider how cybersecurity is evaluated and governed.

Despite this growing awareness, many organizations struggle to integrate cybersecurity into strategic decision making. Security initiatives are often reactive, launched in response to incidents or regulatory pressure rather than guided by long term objectives. Budgets may be allocated without clear understanding of how controls reduce risk or support performance. Security teams may focus on technical vulnerabilities, while business leaders prioritize growth and efficiency, with limited alignment between the two perspectives. This separation creates blind spots where risk accumulates unnoticed.

Viewing cybersecurity as a business imperative requires a shift in mindset. It means recognizing that security decisions influence operational reliability, financial outcomes, and competitive position. Leaders must ask not only whether systems are protected, but how security supports organizational goals. This involves evaluating cyber risk in terms that resonate with business priorities, such as potential revenue loss, downtime, regulatory exposure, and reputational damage. When cybersecurity is framed in this way, it becomes relevant to executive discussions rather than confined to technical reports.

Digital transformation has further amplified the importance of cybersecurity. Organizations are adopting cloud platforms, automation, and data analytics to improve agility and efficiency. These technologies enable new business models and faster decision making, but they also introduce complexity. Systems are interconnected across internal teams, external partners, and geographic boundaries. Data flows continuously between applications and environments. Each connection represents both opportunity and exposure. Security must therefore be embedded into transformation initiatives from the outset, rather than added later as a corrective measure.

Embedding cybersecurity into business processes begins with understanding how value is created and where it is most vulnerable. In many organizations, the most critical assets are not physical infrastructure, but data and the insights derived from it. Financial analytics, customer behavior models, and operational forecasts drive decisions that shape performance. Protecting these assets requires controls that address not only access, but integrity, availability, and appropriate use. Cybersecurity becomes a means of preserving decision quality and organizational confidence.

From a business perspective, cybersecurity also shapes how people interact with systems. Policies, controls, and monitoring mechanisms influence daily behavior. When security measures are poorly designed, they can slow operations, frustrate employees, and encourage unsafe workarounds. When they are aligned with actual workflows, they support efficiency and accountability. Treating cybersecurity as a business imperative involves designing controls that reflect how work is done, rather than imposing rigid rules that conflict with operational reality.

Leadership commitment is central to this alignment. The way executives discuss and prioritize cybersecurity sets expectations across the organization. When leaders engage with security issues thoughtfully, allocate resources deliberately, and hold teams accountable, cybersecurity gains legitimacy. When it is treated as a purely technical concern, it becomes isolated and underfunded. Effective leadership involves asking informed questions, understanding trade offs, and supporting a culture where security is seen as part of professional responsibility.

Governance structures play an important role in reinforcing this perspective. Boards of directors increasingly recognize their responsibility to oversee cyber risk. In regulated industries, board level engagement is often mandated. Directors are expected to understand the organization's risk posture, review management responses, and ensure appropriate controls are in place. This oversight requires translating technical assessments into business relevant information. Metrics, scenarios, and financial models help bridge the gap between security operations and strategic governance.

Regulatory developments further underscore the business imperative of cybersecurity. Data protection laws and industry standards now emphasize accountability and ongoing risk management rather than one time compliance. Organizations must demonstrate that controls are effective and aligned with actual risk exposure. This requires continuous monitoring, documentation, and improvement. Compliance becomes not just a legal obligation, but a reflection of organizational discipline. Enterprises that integrate cybersecurity into governance frameworks are better positioned to meet these expectations.

Cybersecurity also influences competitive dynamics. Trust has become a critical differentiator in markets where data sensitivity is high. Customers and partners are more likely to engage with organizations that demonstrate reliable security practices. Conversely, repeated incidents can erode confidence and drive stakeholders away. In this sense, cybersecurity contributes to brand value and market position. It supports long term relationships by signaling reliability and responsibility.

This does not imply that cybersecurity should be treated as a marketing feature. Rather, it should be embedded authentically into products and services. Secure by design principles reduce risk while enabling innovation. When security considerations inform architecture and process decisions early, they prevent costly rework and disruption later. This proactive approach aligns with business objectives of scalability and sustainability.

Measurement remains a challenge in elevating cybersecurity to a business imperative. Technical indicators such as vulnerability counts or patching timelines do not always convey relevance to non technical stakeholders. Leaders need metrics that connect security performance to outcomes such as reduced downtime, improved compliance, or lower financial exposure. Developing these measures requires collaboration between security teams, finance, and operations. Data analytics plays a key role in translating technical activity into business insight.

Cost considerations further highlight the need for integration. Cybersecurity investments compete with other strategic priorities. Decisions about tools, staffing, and controls involve trade offs. Without a business oriented framework, these decisions may be driven by fear or habit rather than analysis. Viewing cybersecurity as an investment in resilience allows organizations to evaluate options based on risk reduction, cost efficiency, and alignment with goals. This perspective supports more transparent and disciplined decision making.

It is also important to recognize that organizations differ in maturity and resources. Smaller enterprises may lack dedicated security teams, while larger organizations face complexity and legacy systems. In both cases, treating cybersecurity as a business imperative helps prioritize action. Rather than attempting to implement every possible control, organizations can focus on the risks most relevant to their objectives. This prioritization improves effectiveness and reduces unnecessary complexity.

Human factors remain central to cybersecurity outcomes. Employees make decisions every day that affect security, from how they handle data to how they respond to alerts. Training and awareness programs are necessary, but they must be supported by leadership and aligned with business context. When individuals understand how their actions influence organizational outcomes, they are more likely to engage responsibly. Cybersecurity becomes a shared responsibility rather than a specialized function.

As organizations continue to evolve, the importance of cybersecurity as a business imperative will only increase. Digital transformation is ongoing, and new technologies will continue to reshape operations. Threats will adapt, regulations will evolve, and expectations will rise. Organizations that treat cybersecurity as an integral part of strategy will be better equipped to navigate this uncertainty.

Strategic Alignment Between Cybersecurity and Business Objectives

One area that often receives insufficient attention in cybersecurity discussions is the direct alignment between security strategy and business objectives. While many organizations acknowledge the importance of cybersecurity, fewer succeed in embedding it into the mechanisms that guide growth, investment, and competitive positioning. When security operates independently of business planning, it becomes reactive. When it is aligned strategically, it becomes anticipatory and supportive of long term goals.

Strategic alignment begins with recognizing that every major business objective carries an associated digital risk profile. Expansion into new markets introduces data protection and regulatory challenges. The launch of digital products increases exposure to fraud, service disruption, and intellectual property theft. Automation initiatives create dependencies on data integrity and system availability. Cybersecurity must therefore be designed not as a uniform layer applied everywhere, but as a set of controls and capabilities calibrated to what the organization is trying to achieve.

In practice, alignment requires collaboration between security leaders, executives, finance teams, and operational managers. Security priorities should be discussed alongside revenue targets, cost optimization plans, and transformation initiatives. This collaboration enables organizations to identify where security investment delivers the greatest value. It also prevents situations where security controls unintentionally obstruct critical business processes or delay strategic initiatives.

Strategic alignment also reshapes how success is measured. Instead of focusing solely on incident counts or compliance status, organizations can assess how cybersecurity contributes to stability, continuity, and decision quality. For example, reduced downtime during peak operations, faster recovery from disruptions, or improved confidence in financial reporting all represent tangible business outcomes influenced by security posture. When these outcomes are visible, cybersecurity gains legitimacy as a strategic function.

Another important aspect of alignment is timing. Security considerations introduced late in a project often result in costly redesigns or compromised controls. When security is involved early, it informs architecture, vendor selection, and process design. This proactive involvement reduces friction and supports innovation rather than constraining it. In digitally competitive markets, the ability to move quickly without sacrificing reliability is a significant advantage.

Alignment also affects organizational culture. When cybersecurity is positioned as a shared enabler rather than an external constraint, employees are more likely to engage constructively. They understand that security supports their ability to deliver results safely and consistently. This perspective encourages responsible behavior and reduces the tendency to bypass controls for convenience.

Case Study: Cybersecurity Supporting Digital Expansion in a Financial Services Firm

Consider a mid sized financial services firm undergoing rapid digital expansion. The organization planned to introduce mobile platforms, automated credit assessment, and data driven customer insights to compete more effectively in a crowded market. Initially, cybersecurity was treated as a compliance requirement, addressed primarily through audits and documentation.

As digital initiatives progressed, several challenges emerged. Transaction volumes increased, third party integrations multiplied, and customer data began flowing across new channels. At the same time, leadership became concerned about fraud exposure, service reliability, and regulatory scrutiny. Isolated security controls were no longer sufficient to manage these risks.

In response, the firm reassessed its approach and repositioned cybersecurity as a strategic partner to the business. Security leaders were included in transformation planning sessions and worked closely with product, finance, and compliance teams. Together, they identified critical business objectives and mapped associated digital risks. This exercise revealed that the most significant threats were not external attacks alone, but data inconsistencies, delayed detection of anomalies, and limited visibility across systems.

To address these issues, the firm invested in data driven security analytics integrated with core business platforms. Transaction monitoring systems were enhanced to detect behavioral patterns indicative of fraud. Access controls were redesigned to align with operational roles rather than rigid technical categories. Automated reporting provided executives with clear visibility into risk exposure during peak business periods.

The impact of this alignment was measurable. Fraud losses declined as anomalies were detected earlier. System availability improved during high demand cycles. Regulatory reviews became more efficient due to consistent and transparent controls. Perhaps most importantly, leadership gained confidence that digital expansion could proceed without introducing unmanaged risk.

Cybersecurity as a Driver of Operational Resilience and Continuity

Beyond strategy and growth, one of the most critical roles cybersecurity plays in modern organizations is enabling operational resilience. Resilience refers to an organization's ability to continue functioning under stress, recover quickly from disruption, and adapt to changing conditions without significant loss of performance or trust. In an era where digital systems underpin nearly every operational process, cybersecurity is a central determinant of whether resilience is theoretical or real.

Operational resilience is often misunderstood as disaster recovery or business continuity planning alone. While those elements are important, they represent only a portion of the challenge. True resilience depends on the reliability of systems during normal operations, not just during crises. It requires visibility into how systems behave, how data flows, and how quickly anomalies can be detected and addressed. Cybersecurity provides the mechanisms through which this visibility and control are achieved.

Many disruptions attributed to cyber incidents are not sudden catastrophes. They begin as small failures. Delayed alerts, misconfigured access rights, inconsistent data feeds, or unmonitored integrations gradually weaken system reliability. Over time, these weaknesses accumulate until a triggering event causes widespread disruption. Cybersecurity, when treated as a business imperative, focuses on preventing this slow erosion of control by embedding safeguards into daily operations.

Resilience also depends on decision quality under pressure. During disruptions, leaders must assess impact, prioritize actions, and communicate clearly. If data integrity is compromised or system status is unclear, decision making suffers. Cybersecurity practices that emphasize data accuracy, auditability, and real time monitoring support faster and more confident responses. In this way, security directly influences how effectively organizations manage uncertainty.

Another important dimension of resilience is dependency management. Modern enterprises rely on complex ecosystems of vendors, platforms, and partners. Cloud services, payment processors, analytics tools, and application programming interfaces are deeply integrated into operations. While these dependencies enable efficiency and scalability, they also expand the attack surface. Cybersecurity must therefore extend beyond internal systems to include third party risk and supply chain visibility. Without this broader view, resilience remains fragile.

Operational resilience is also closely tied to cost control. Disruptions are expensive. Downtime leads to lost revenue, emergency remediation costs, and potential penalties. Even short interruptions can have outsized financial impact in high volume or time sensitive environments. Cybersecurity investments that reduce the frequency, duration, or severity of disruptions contribute directly to cost efficiency. When resilience is improved, organizations spend less time reacting and more time executing strategy.

Importantly, resilience is not achieved through rigid control alone. Overly restrictive security measures can slow response and create bottlenecks. Effective cybersecurity balances protection with flexibility. It enables rapid adaptation while maintaining oversight. This balance is especially important in digitally transformed operations where automation and real time decision making are central to performance.

Case Study: Strengthening Operational Resilience in a Digitally Integrated Manufacturing Enterprise

A large manufacturing enterprise provides a useful illustration of how cybersecurity supports operational resilience. The organization had invested heavily in digital integration across its production facilities, supply chain management systems, and analytics platforms. Sensors monitored equipment performance, automated systems optimized inventory levels, and data dashboards informed operational decisions. While these capabilities improved efficiency, they also increased reliance on continuous data availability and system integrity.

Initially, cybersecurity was addressed primarily through perimeter defenses and periodic audits. Internal systems were assumed to be reliable once deployed. Over time, however, the organization experienced a series of operational disruptions. Production lines halted unexpectedly due to data synchronization issues. Inventory systems reported conflicting information across locations. Maintenance decisions were delayed because analytics outputs could not be trusted during critical moments.

Investigations revealed that these disruptions were not caused by dramatic cyber attacks, but by gradual control failures. Access privileges were inconsistent across systems. Monitoring focused on external threats while internal anomalies went unnoticed. Data pipelines lacked validation checks, allowing errors to propagate through analytics platforms. Cybersecurity had been implemented as a protective layer, not as an operational discipline.

Recognizing the impact on productivity and cost, leadership reframed cybersecurity as a resilience initiative rather than a compliance function. Security teams collaborated with operations, engineering, and finance to identify points of dependency and failure across digital workflows. The focus shifted from preventing breaches alone to ensuring system reliability and data integrity under normal and stressed conditions.

The organization implemented integrated monitoring that correlated security events with operational metrics. Data validation controls were embedded into analytics pipelines to detect inconsistencies early. Access management was redesigned to reflect operational roles, reducing errors caused by inappropriate permissions. Incident response processes were aligned with production priorities, enabling faster resolution when issues arose.

The results were significant. Unplanned downtime decreased as issues were identified earlier. Decision confidence improved because analytics outputs were more reliable. Maintenance schedules became more accurate, reducing equipment failure rates. From a financial perspective, the organization saw measurable reductions in disruption related costs and improved predictability in production output.

Perhaps most importantly, cybersecurity became part of operational planning. Security considerations were included when new systems were introduced or processes redesigned. Rather than reacting to failures, the organization developed the ability to anticipate and absorb disruption. Cybersecurity evolved from a protective function into a stabilizing force within daily operations.

This case underscores a critical insight. Operational resilience is not achieved through isolated controls or emergency plans. It emerges from the consistent application of cybersecurity principles across systems, data, and decision processes. When cybersecurity is treated as a business imperative, it strengthens the organization's ability to withstand disruption, manage complexity, and operate with confidence.

Chapter 2

Foundations of Secure Digital Architecture

Every discussion about cybersecurity eventually returns to one fundamental question: how are digital systems built in the first place? Before threats can be detected, risks quantified, or incidents managed, there must be an underlying architecture that determines how data moves, how systems interact, and how control is enforced. Secure digital architecture is the foundation upon which all effective cybersecurity strategies rest. Without it, even the most advanced tools struggle to deliver meaningful protection.

Digital architecture refers to the structure of systems, networks, applications, and data flows that support organizational operations. It defines boundaries, dependencies, and points of control. When architecture is designed without security in mind, vulnerabilities are often embedded deeply and become difficult to correct later. When security is integrated at the architectural level, organizations gain resilience, visibility, and scalability.

Historically, many systems were designed in relatively closed environments. Networks were centralized, users were known, and data rarely moved beyond organizational boundaries. Security models reflected this reality, relying heavily on perimeter defenses and internal trust. Modern enterprises operate very differently. Cloud services, remote work, third party integrations, and application programming interfaces have dissolved traditional boundaries. Architecture must now assume constant connectivity and persistent risk.

The foundation of secure digital architecture begins with clear principles. These principles guide design decisions and ensure consistency across systems. One of the most enduring is the principle of least privilege. Users and systems should have access only to what is necessary to perform their functions. Excessive access increases exposure and magnifies the impact of compromise. Implementing least privilege requires understanding roles, workflows, and dependencies, which reinforces the need for collaboration between technical and business teams.

Another foundational principle is defense in depth. No single control should be relied upon as the sole barrier to attack. Instead, multiple layers of protection work together to reduce risk. These layers may include network segmentation, identity controls, encryption, monitoring, and response mechanisms. When one layer fails, others remain in place. This approach acknowledges that failures are inevitable and focuses on limiting their consequences.

Data centric security has also become central to modern architecture. As data flows across systems and environments, protecting it solely at the perimeter is no longer effective. Secure architectures emphasize protecting data wherever it resides and however it is used. Encryption, integrity checks, and access controls tied directly to data assets help ensure confidentiality and reliability. This approach aligns security with how value is created and decisions are made.

Identity has emerged as a critical control point in digital architecture. Users, applications, and services all require identity to interact. Weak identity management undermines even the strongest technical controls. Secure architectures treat identity as a core component rather than an add on. Authentication, authorization, and continuous verification ensure that access decisions reflect current context and risk. This shift supports more flexible operations without sacrificing control.

Architectural foundations also influence how organizations respond to change. Digital environments evolve rapidly. New applications are deployed, integrations are added, and workflows are modified. Secure architecture provides a framework for accommodating change without introducing unmanaged risk. Standardized interfaces, clear trust boundaries, and consistent control mechanisms make adaptation safer and more predictable.

One of the most significant architectural shifts in recent years has been the move to cloud based infrastructure. Cloud environments offer scalability and efficiency, but they also require new approaches to security. Responsibility is shared between service providers and customers. Secure architecture in the cloud demands clarity about roles, visibility into configurations, and continuous monitoring. Organizations must design architectures that leverage cloud capabilities while maintaining accountability for security outcomes.

Secure digital architecture also plays a critical role in supporting data analytics and automation. As organizations rely more heavily on analytics for decision making, the integrity and availability of data become essential. Architectures that include validation checks, audit trails, and monitoring support reliable analytics. They reduce the risk of decisions being based on corrupted or incomplete information. This connection between architecture and decision quality is often overlooked, yet it is central to business performance.

Another important consideration is interoperability. Modern enterprises rarely operate with a single technology stack. Mergers, partnerships, and vendor ecosystems introduce diversity. Secure architecture provides a common framework for integrating disparate systems without compromising control. Standardized security patterns and shared governance principles help manage complexity.

The cost of poor architectural decisions can be substantial. Retrofitting security controls into systems not designed for them is expensive and disruptive. It often requires downtime, redesign, and cultural adjustment. In contrast, investing in secure architecture early reduces long term cost and risk. It enables incremental improvement rather than reactive overhaul. This cost efficiency reinforces the business case for architectural discipline.

Human factors also influence architectural effectiveness. Systems are designed and operated by people. Complexity increases the likelihood of error. Secure architectures aim to simplify where possible and make correct behavior the default. Automation, clear interfaces, and sensible defaults reduce reliance on individual judgment for routine security decisions. This approach improves consistency and reduces operational risk.

A technology services company transitioning to a cloud native model illustrates the importance of secure digital architecture. The organization sought to modernize its operations by migrating applications to the cloud, introducing microservices, and enabling remote collaboration. Speed was a priority, as competitive pressure demanded rapid delivery of new features.

Initially, the migration focused on functionality and performance. Applications were moved quickly, and integrations were established to support business needs. Security controls were added incrementally, often mirroring legacy approaches. Over time, issues emerged. Access permissions were inconsistent. Monitoring lacked visibility across services. Data moved between components without adequate validation. While no major breach occurred, leadership recognized growing exposure.

The organization paused its migration and reassessed its architectural approach. Security architects worked with development and operations teams to define clear principles. Identity became the primary control point, with centralized authentication and role based access aligned to business functions. Network segmentation was implemented to limit lateral movement between services. Data encryption and integrity checks were standardized across platforms.

Equally important, the architecture incorporated monitoring and logging as core components rather than optional features. Security and operational data were collected centrally, enabling correlation and analysis. Automation was introduced to enforce configuration standards and detect deviations in real time. These changes required effort, but they also reduced manual intervention and error.

As the new architecture matured, benefits became evident. Deployment velocity improved because teams worked within clear guardrails. Incident response became faster due to improved visibility. Compliance reporting was simplified because controls were consistent and auditable. From a business perspective, the organization gained confidence that growth could continue without introducing disproportionate risk.

Architectural Governance and Accountability in Secure Systems

An often overlooked component of secure digital architecture is governance. While architecture is frequently discussed in terms of technology and design patterns, its effectiveness ultimately depends on how decisions are governed, reviewed, and enforced over time. Without governance, even well designed architectures degrade as systems evolve, teams change, and priorities shift.

Architectural governance establishes who is responsible for security related decisions, how those decisions are evaluated, and how consistency is maintained across the organization. In secure systems, governance is not about control for its own sake. It is about ensuring that architectural choices align with organizational risk tolerance, regulatory obligations, and operational realities. When governance is absent or weak, security decisions become fragmented, leading to inconsistent implementations and unmanaged exposure.

One key aspect of governance is decision ownership. Secure digital architecture requires clarity on who approves system designs, integrations, and changes that affect security posture. In many organizations, architectural decisions are distributed across teams without a unifying framework. This can result in duplicated controls in some areas and gaps in others. Effective governance defines escalation paths, review processes, and accountability structures that ensure security implications are considered consistently.

Governance also supports architectural discipline over time. Systems rarely remain static. New features are added, vendors are integrated, and processes are modified to support business needs. Each change introduces potential risk. Governance mechanisms such as design reviews, change approval processes, and periodic reassessment help ensure that security principles continue to be applied as systems evolve. This continuity is critical for maintaining long term resilience.

Another important function of architectural governance is alignment with organizational strategy. Security controls should reflect business priorities and risk appetite. For example, systems supporting core revenue functions may require stronger controls and higher availability than internal support tools. Governance frameworks help translate these priorities into architectural standards. This prevents a one size fits all approach and enables more efficient allocation of resources.

Governance also plays a role in transparency. Clear documentation of architectural decisions, assumptions, and trade offs improves understanding across teams. It allows leaders to assess risk more accurately and supports audit and compliance efforts. When decisions are documented and traceable, organizations are better positioned to explain why certain controls exist and how they support business objectives.

In secure digital architecture, governance is not a barrier to innovation. When implemented thoughtfully, it provides guardrails rather than rigid constraints. Teams gain clarity about acceptable patterns and are empowered to innovate within defined boundaries. This balance supports agility while reducing the likelihood of costly rework or security failures.

Resilience Through Redundancy, Segmentation, and Fail Safe Design

Another critical dimension of secure digital architecture is the deliberate design for failure. No system is immune to disruption. Hardware fails, software contains defects, and human error is inevitable. Secure architecture therefore must assume that components will fail and focus on limiting the impact of those failures. This approach shifts the emphasis from prevention alone to resilience and continuity.

Redundancy is a foundational concept in this context. By providing multiple pathways or components to perform essential functions, architectures reduce single points of failure. Redundancy can exist at many levels, including infrastructure, data storage, authentication services, and monitoring systems. When designed properly, redundancy ensures that disruptions do not immediately translate into outages or loss of control.

Segmentation complements redundancy by limiting the spread of failures. In segmented architectures, systems are divided into zones based on function, sensitivity, or risk. Access between zones is controlled and monitored. This design reduces the likelihood that a failure or compromise in one area will propagate across the entire environment. Segmentation is especially important in complex organizations where diverse systems coexist.

Fail safe design extends these concepts by defining how systems behave when things go wrong. Rather than defaulting to permissive or undefined states, secure architectures specify controlled responses to failure. For example, access may be restricted when authentication services are unavailable, or transactions may be paused when data integrity cannot be verified. These responses prioritize safety and control over convenience.

From a business perspective, resilience through architectural design reduces uncertainty. Leaders gain confidence that systems can absorb shocks without catastrophic impact. This confidence supports more ambitious transformation initiatives because risk is managed proactively rather than reactively. Resilient architecture also improves recovery time, reducing downtime and associated financial loss.

Fail safe design also supports regulatory expectations around operational resilience. Regulators increasingly focus on how organizations prepare for disruption, not just how they prevent incidents. Architectures that demonstrate clear containment, recovery, and control mechanisms align well with these expectations. This reduces compliance risk and strengthens stakeholder confidence.

Importantly, designing for resilience requires trade offs. Redundancy and segmentation introduce cost and complexity. Secure digital architecture involves making deliberate choices about where these investments deliver the greatest value. By grounding these decisions in business impact and risk assessment, organizations can achieve resilience without unnecessary overhead.

Together, architectural governance and resilience oriented design deepen the foundation established earlier in this chapter. They shift secure digital architecture from a static blueprint to a living system that adapts, absorbs disruption, and supports long term business objectives. These elements prepare organizations to confront evolving threats, which becomes the focus of the next chapter.

Chapter 3

The Evolving Cyber Threat Landscape

Cyber threats do not exist in isolation from the environments they target. They evolve in response to technology, business practices, and human behavior. As organizations digitize operations, automate decisions, and rely more heavily on interconnected systems, adversaries adapt their methods to exploit new dependencies and weaknesses. Understanding the modern cyber threat landscape therefore requires more than cataloging attack types. It requires examining how threats emerge, why they succeed, and how they align with organizational vulnerabilities.

In earlier eras, cyber threats were often opportunistic. Attackers exploited widely known vulnerabilities, targeted exposed systems, and sought disruption or notoriety. Today's threats are more deliberate and strategic. Many attacks are financially motivated, designed to extract value through fraud, extortion, or intellectual property theft. Others are aimed at long term access, surveillance, or influence. This shift reflects the increasing value of data and the central role digital systems play in economic activity.

One defining feature of the modern threat landscape is persistence. Advanced adversaries do not rely on single entry points or rapid exploitation alone. They invest time in understanding target environments, mapping dependencies, and identifying weak signals. Once access is gained, they may remain undetected for extended periods, observing behavior and waiting for opportunities to escalate impact. This persistence challenges traditional security models that focus on perimeter defense and signature based detection.

Another important development is the targeting of business processes rather than technology alone. Cyber adversaries increasingly exploit how organizations operate. They manipulate workflows, exploit trust relationships, and take advantage of automation logic. For example, attacks may target approval processes, payment systems, or data pipelines to influence outcomes without triggering obvious technical alarms. These methods blur the line between cyber risk and operational risk, reinforcing the need for integrated security approaches.

The growth of interconnected ecosystems has also expanded the threat surface. Organizations depend on vendors, partners, and service providers for critical functions. Each integration introduces new pathways for attack. Supply chain compromises illustrate how adversaries can exploit trusted relationships to gain access to multiple targets simultaneously. In such scenarios, the security posture of one organization affects many others. Managing this risk requires visibility beyond internal systems.

Human behavior remains a central factor in the threat landscape. Social engineering attacks exploit trust, urgency, and authority rather than technical flaws. Phishing, impersonation, and manipulation tactics continue to succeed because they target cognitive biases and organizational culture. As digital interactions increase and remote work becomes more common, opportunities for deception expand. Cybersecurity strategies must therefore address not only systems, but also how people interact with them.

Automation and artificial intelligence have influenced both defensive and offensive capabilities. Adversaries use automation to scale attacks, test vulnerabilities, and adapt tactics quickly. Automated tools can generate convincing messages, probe systems continuously, and exploit weaknesses at speed. At the same time, defenders deploy automation to monitor environments, detect anomalies, and respond more rapidly. This dynamic creates an ongoing contest where advantage depends on insight, adaptability, and coordination rather than static controls.

Data integrity has emerged as a critical concern within the evolving threat landscape. Attacks that alter data without obvious disruption can undermine decision making in subtle but damaging ways. Corrupted analytics, manipulated transaction records, or skewed reporting outputs may not trigger immediate alarms, yet they influence strategic choices. Such attacks target confidence rather than availability, making them particularly difficult to detect and assess.

The financial dimension of cyber threats has also become more pronounced. Ransomware attacks, payment fraud, and market manipulation directly affect revenue and cash flow. Attackers understand business cycles, peak operational periods, and regulatory deadlines. They time attacks to maximize leverage and pressure. This awareness reinforces the importance of aligning cybersecurity with financial analytics and risk management.

Regulatory and geopolitical factors further shape the threat environment. Regulations influence attacker incentives by defining penalties and disclosure requirements. Geopolitical tensions can motivate espionage and sabotage activities targeting critical infrastructure and strategic industries. Organizations operating across borders must navigate varying threat profiles and legal obligations. Cybersecurity strategies that fail to account for these contextual factors risk being misaligned with reality.

Another evolving aspect of the threat landscape is complexity. As systems grow more intricate, unintended interactions create opportunities for exploitation. Misconfigurations, inconsistent controls, and unclear ownership increase risk. Adversaries often exploit these gaps rather than breaking through strong defenses directly. Complexity itself becomes a vulnerability, emphasizing the importance of architectural discipline and governance discussed in earlier chapters.

Threat intelligence plays a crucial role in understanding this landscape. However, intelligence must be interpreted carefully. Generic threat reports provide awareness, but they do not replace contextual analysis. Organizations must assess how threats relate to their specific assets, processes, and dependencies. Effective threat understanding combines external intelligence with internal data, operational insight, and business context.

Importantly, the evolving threat landscape challenges the assumption that prevention alone is sufficient. No organization can eliminate all risk. Instead, emphasis must shift toward early detection, rapid response, and recovery. This requires visibility, analytics, and coordination across teams. Cybersecurity becomes an ongoing practice rather than a static state.

Leadership awareness is essential in navigating this environment. Executives and boards must understand that cyber threats are not abstract technical issues. They are business realities that influence strategy, investment, and reputation. Informed leadership enables organizations to allocate resources wisely, prioritize risk, and support resilience.

Threat Evolution Driven by Business Digitization

One of the most important forces shaping the modern cyber threat landscape is business digitization itself. As organizations digitize core processes, adversaries adjust their methods to align with where value is created and controlled. Cyber threats today mirror business architecture more closely than technical architecture. Attackers study how organizations generate revenue, authorize transactions, manage data, and automate decisions, then design attacks that exploit these pathways.

Digitization increases efficiency by reducing human intervention and accelerating workflows. At the same time, it concentrates authority within systems. Automated approvals, algorithmic decision engines, and centralized data platforms reduce friction but also reduce tolerance for error. A single compromised process can have cascading effects across departments, financial records, and customer interactions. Threat actors understand this concentration and target it deliberately.

This evolution explains why modern attacks often focus on manipulation rather than destruction. Instead of disabling systems outright, attackers may alter inputs, influence analytics outputs, or redirect automated actions. These techniques are harder to detect because systems continue operating. Business leaders may not realize they are responding to compromised data until consequences become visible in financial results or compliance failures.

Digitization also shortens the time between action and impact. In highly automated environments, malicious changes propagate quickly. Decisions are executed before anomalies are reviewed. This dynamic forces organizations to rethink detection strategies. Traditional periodic reviews and manual oversight are insufficient. Threat evolution driven by digitization demands continuous validation, anomaly detection, and architectural safeguards that assume compromise is possible.

Understanding this relationship between business digitization and threat behavior is essential. Cybersecurity strategies that focus only on technical vulnerabilities fail to address how attackers exploit business logic. Effective defense requires analyzing how systems support decisions, how automation enforces rules, and where assumptions may be abused.

The Blurring Boundary Between Cyber Threats and Operational Risk

Another defining feature of the evolving threat landscape is the erosion of clear boundaries between cyber threats and operational risk. In modern enterprises, digital systems are embedded in operational workflows to such an extent that cyber incidents manifest as operational failures rather than technical events. This convergence complicates detection, response, and accountability.

For example, when a data pipeline delivers inaccurate outputs due to manipulation or error, the resulting decisions may disrupt operations, misallocate resources, or violate regulations. The root cause may be cyber in nature, but the symptoms appear operational. As a result, responsibility may be fragmented across teams, delaying response and obscuring lessons learned.

This blurring of boundaries challenges traditional organizational structures. Security teams may focus on intrusion detection and access control, while operations teams manage performance and reliability. When threats exploit operational dependencies, neither group has full visibility. Cybersecurity must therefore be integrated into operational risk management rather than treated as a separate discipline.

The convergence also affects how incidents are measured. Traditional metrics such as breach counts or system downtime do not capture the full impact of cyber enabled operational disruption. Organizations must develop new indicators that reflect decision accuracy, process integrity, and service reliability. These metrics provide a more accurate picture of risk in digitally integrated environments.

Recognizing cyber threats as operational risk drivers shifts the emphasis from isolated controls to systemic resilience. It encourages collaboration across security, operations, finance, and compliance functions. This integrated perspective is essential for managing threats that exploit complexity rather than obvious technical weaknesses.

Threat Acceleration Through Automation and Scale

Automation has transformed both defensive and offensive cyber capabilities. For defenders, automation enables continuous monitoring, rapid response, and consistency across environments. For adversaries, it enables scale. Attacks that once required manual effort can now be executed simultaneously across thousands of targets. This acceleration fundamentally alters the threat landscape.

Automated attack tools can scan for vulnerabilities, test credentials, and adapt tactics with minimal human intervention. These tools operate continuously, exploiting short windows of opportunity created by misconfigurations or delayed patches. The speed at which attacks occur reduces the margin for error. Organizations that rely on manual detection and response are at a disadvantage.

Scale also increases noise. Automated attacks generate large volumes of low level activity, making it difficult to distinguish serious threats from background scanning. This environment challenges security teams to prioritize effectively. Without data driven filtering and contextual analysis, critical signals may be missed.

Acceleration through automation also changes attacker economics. Low cost, high volume attacks make it feasible to target a broader range of organizations, including those previously considered unattractive. As a result, no organization can assume it is too small or obscure to be targeted. The threat landscape becomes more democratic, with exposure determined by connectivity rather than prominence.

For defenders, this acceleration reinforces the need for intelligent automation governed by strategy. Automation must be guided by clear priorities and supported by oversight. Without governance, automated defenses risk responding incorrectly or amplifying errors. The evolving threat landscape therefore demands not just faster tools, but better integration between automation, analytics, and decision making.

Chapter 4

AI Powered Cybersecurity Automation

Cybersecurity has reached a point where human driven processes alone can no longer keep pace with the volume, speed, and complexity of modern threats. As organizations expand digital operations, generate vast amounts of data, and rely on interconnected systems, the scale of activity exceeds what manual monitoring and response can effectively manage. Artificial intelligence has therefore emerged not as a supplementary tool, but as a structural necessity in cybersecurity operations.

AI powered cybersecurity automation refers to the use of machine learning, statistical modeling, and intelligent decision systems to detect threats, analyze behavior, and initiate responses with minimal human intervention. This approach does not replace security professionals. Instead, it augments their capacity by handling repetitive tasks, identifying subtle patterns, and accelerating response times. In doing so, it reshapes how cybersecurity functions within the enterprise.

At its core, AI driven security focuses on learning. Traditional security tools rely heavily on predefined rules and known signatures. While effective against familiar threats, these methods struggle to detect novel or adaptive attacks. AI systems learn from historical data and ongoing activity, enabling them to identify deviations from expected behavior. This capability is particularly valuable in environments where threats exploit business logic rather than obvious vulnerabilities.

Automation also addresses one of the most persistent challenges in cybersecurity: alert fatigue. Security teams often face overwhelming volumes of alerts, many of which are false positives or low priority events. AI systems can correlate signals across multiple data sources, assess context, and rank alerts based on risk. This prioritization allows human analysts to focus on issues that require judgment and strategic decision making.

Another important dimension of AI powered automation is consistency. Human responses vary based on experience, workload, and stress. Automated systems apply policies uniformly, reducing the likelihood of oversight or inconsistency. This is especially important in large organizations with distributed teams and complex infrastructures. Consistent enforcement supports both security and compliance objectives.

AI driven automation also enables faster containment and recovery. When threats are detected early, automated responses can isolate affected systems, revoke access, or initiate remediation steps before damage spreads. Speed is critical. Many attacks escalate quickly, and delays increase impact. Automated response mechanisms reduce the time between detection and action, strengthening resilience.

However, automation introduces new considerations. AI systems must be trained on accurate and representative data. Poor data quality leads to unreliable outputs. Bias in training data can skew detection, causing certain behaviors to be misclassified. Governance is therefore essential. Organizations must define how models are trained, evaluated, and updated to ensure reliability and fairness.

Explainability is another important factor. Security decisions often have significant consequences, including system shutdowns or regulatory implications. Stakeholders need to understand why actions were taken. AI systems that provide interpretable outputs support trust and accountability. This transparency is especially important when automation intersects with compliance and financial reporting.

AI powered cybersecurity automation also changes the skill requirements within security teams. Professionals must understand how models work, how to interpret outputs, and how to intervene when necessary. This shift emphasizes analytical thinking and system oversight rather than manual execution. Training and organizational culture must evolve accordingly.

From a business perspective, AI driven security supports scalability. As operations grow, security capabilities can expand without proportional increases in staff. This scalability enables organizations to pursue digital transformation initiatives with greater confidence. Security becomes an enabler rather than a bottleneck.

It is important to recognize that automation is not a single technology, but a layered capability. It includes data ingestion, feature extraction, model training, inference, and response orchestration. Each layer must be designed and governed carefully. Weaknesses in any layer undermine the effectiveness of the whole.

AI powered automation also intersects with other domains such as financial analytics and risk management. Threat detection can be informed by transaction patterns, user behavior, and operational metrics. This integration strengthens situational awareness and supports more informed decision making. Cybersecurity becomes part of a broader analytical ecosystem.

As threats continue to evolve, static defenses will become increasingly ineffective. AI powered cybersecurity automation provides the adaptability and speed required to respond to dynamic environments. When implemented thoughtfully, it enhances protection, reduces operational burden, and supports strategic objectives.

Behavioral Analytics and Anomaly Detection at Scale

One of the most transformative applications of artificial intelligence in cybersecurity automation is behavioral analytics. Rather than focusing solely on known threat indicators, behavioral analytics establishes patterns of normal activity across users, systems, and data flows, then identifies deviations that may indicate malicious intent or system misuse. This approach is particularly effective in modern environments where threats are subtle, adaptive, and embedded within legitimate workflows.

Behavioral analytics operates by continuously observing how entities interact with systems. These entities may include users, applications, devices, or services. By analyzing variables such as access frequency, timing, transaction patterns, and data usage, AI models build contextual baselines. These baselines are dynamic. They evolve as roles change, workloads shift, and systems scale. This adaptability allows detection mechanisms to remain relevant over time.

Anomaly detection at scale addresses one of the key challenges faced by security teams: distinguishing meaningful risk from routine variability. In large organizations, thousands of deviations occur daily. Not all deviations are threats. AI systems evaluate anomalies in context, considering historical behavior, peer group comparisons, and operational conditions. This contextual evaluation reduces false positives and improves confidence in alerts.

Behavioral analytics also enhances detection of insider risk and compromised credentials. Traditional security controls often assume that authenticated users are legitimate. Behavioral analysis challenges this assumption by monitoring how access is used. Unusual data access patterns, atypical transaction timing, or deviations in workflow execution can signal risk even when credentials are valid. This capability is critical in environments where attackers leverage stolen identities rather than technical exploits.

From an operational standpoint, anomaly detection supports proactive risk management. Instead of reacting to incidents after damage occurs, organizations can intervene earlier. Subtle indicators are surfaced before escalation. This early warning capability aligns with business objectives related to continuity, trust, and cost control.

Behavioral analytics also benefits from integration with non security data. Financial metrics, operational logs, and performance indicators provide additional context. When analytics correlate behavior across domains, detection becomes more precise. This integration reinforces the role of AI powered cybersecurity as part of an enterprise wide intelligence framework rather than a standalone function.

Automated Response Orchestration and Decision Support

Detection alone does not prevent impact. The value of AI powered cybersecurity automation is realized when insights translate into timely and appropriate action. Automated response orchestration coordinates predefined actions across systems based on detected risk, enabling rapid containment and mitigation. This capability reduces dependence on manual intervention during critical moments.

Response orchestration involves mapping potential threats to response strategies. These strategies may include isolating systems, revoking access, enforcing additional authentication, or triggering investigation workflows. AI systems assess severity and context to select appropriate actions. This decision support function ensures that responses are proportionate and aligned with policy.

One advantage of automated response is speed. Many attacks unfold within minutes. Automated actions reduce latency between detection and containment. This speed limits damage and reduces recovery time. For organizations with global operations or limited security staffing, automation provides consistent coverage across time zones and environments.

Decision support is equally important. Not all situations warrant automated containment. Some require human judgment. AI systems can present recommendations with supporting context, allowing analysts to approve or modify actions. This hybrid approach balances efficiency with control. It preserves human oversight while reducing cognitive load.

Automated response orchestration also supports learning. Outcomes of actions can be fed back into models to improve future decisions. This feedback loop enhances accuracy over time. It allows systems to adapt to organizational priorities and evolving threat patterns.

Governance remains essential in automated response. Clear policies define which actions are permitted, under what conditions, and with what safeguards. Oversight mechanisms ensure accountability and prevent unintended consequences. When governance is embedded into orchestration design, automation becomes a trusted extension of security operations rather than a risk in itself.

From a strategic perspective, automated response aligns cybersecurity with business resilience. It enables organizations to absorb shocks, maintain service levels, and recover quickly. By reducing reliance on ad hoc reactions, it supports disciplined and repeatable incident management.

Together, behavioral analytics and response orchestration illustrate how AI powered automation extends beyond detection. It creates an integrated system capable of learning, deciding, and acting at scale.

Chapter 5

Data Driven Threat Intelligence and Predictive Security

Modern cybersecurity is no longer defined by reaction alone. As digital environments grow more complex, organizations must anticipate threats before they materialize into incidents. Data driven threat intelligence provides the foundation for this shift by transforming raw security data into insight that supports foresight, prioritization, and strategic decision making. Predictive security builds on this intelligence, enabling organizations to move from defensive posture to proactive control.

Threat intelligence begins with data. Logs, alerts, network activity, user behavior, transaction records, and external intelligence feeds all contribute signals about potential risk. Individually, these signals offer limited value. Their true power emerges when they are aggregated, contextualized, and analyzed systematically. Data driven threat intelligence focuses on extracting meaning from this complexity.

A key distinction between traditional threat intelligence and data driven approaches is relevance. Generic threat reports describe trends and known attack techniques, but they often lack applicability to specific environments. Data driven intelligence incorporates internal context such as system architecture, business processes, and asset criticality. This alignment allows organizations to assess which threats matter most and why.

Predictive security extends this concept by using historical patterns and behavioral indicators to forecast potential future events. Rather than waiting for indicators of compromise, predictive models identify conditions that increase risk. For example, combinations of configuration changes, access behavior, and system load may signal heightened vulnerability. By recognizing these patterns early, organizations can intervene before exploitation occurs.

Data quality is central to effective threat intelligence. Incomplete, inconsistent, or poorly structured data undermines analysis. Organizations must invest in data governance practices that ensure accuracy, timeliness, and integrity. This includes standardizing data formats, validating sources, and managing retention. High quality data supports more reliable intelligence and reduces noise.

Correlation is another critical capability. Threats rarely manifest as single events. They unfold across time and systems. Data driven intelligence correlates signals across domains, linking seemingly unrelated activities into coherent narratives. This holistic view reveals attack progression and intent. Correlation also supports prioritization by highlighting sequences that indicate escalation.

Predictive models rely on continuous learning. As environments and threat behaviors change, models must adapt. Feedback loops allow systems to refine predictions based on outcomes. This adaptability distinguishes predictive security from static risk assessments. It enables organizations to remain responsive in dynamic conditions.

Threat intelligence also informs resource allocation. By identifying likely attack vectors and high risk assets, organizations can focus investment where it delivers the greatest impact. This strategic use of intelligence supports cost efficiency and aligns cybersecurity with business objectives.

Another important dimension of data driven threat intelligence is collaboration. Intelligence gains value when shared appropriately. Internal collaboration between security, operations, and business teams improves understanding and response. External collaboration with trusted partners and industry groups enhances situational awareness. Data driven approaches support this exchange by providing structured, evidence based insight.

Predictive security does not eliminate uncertainty. Models produce probabilities, not certainties. Decision makers must interpret predictions within context. Transparency and explainability support trust in these insights. When stakeholders understand how predictions are generated, they are more likely to act on them.

From a governance perspective, predictive security introduces accountability considerations. Decisions influenced by models must be traceable. Organizations must document assumptions, thresholds, and response strategies. This documentation supports auditability and regulatory expectations.

Data driven threat intelligence also intersects with financial analytics and risk management. Threat likelihood and impact can be quantified and incorporated into enterprise risk models. This integration enables more informed discussions at leadership level. Cybersecurity risk becomes comparable with other strategic risks rather than an abstract technical concern.

Integrating Threat Intelligence into Strategic Decision Making

While data driven threat intelligence is often discussed in technical terms, its true value is realized when it informs strategic decision making at the organizational level. Cybersecurity intelligence should not exist solely within security operations centers or analyst dashboards. It must influence how leaders allocate resources, design processes, and assess risk across the enterprise.

Strategic decision making requires clarity, prioritization, and context. Threat intelligence provides these elements by translating complex technical signals into risk narratives that align with business objectives. When intelligence highlights which assets are most exposed, which attack vectors are most likely, and which consequences carry the greatest impact, leaders can make informed trade offs rather than reactive decisions.

One important aspect of this integration is risk prioritization. Not all threats are equal, and not all vulnerabilities warrant immediate action. Data driven intelligence enables organizations to rank risks based on likelihood and potential impact. This prioritization supports rational investment decisions, ensuring that security budgets are directed toward controls that reduce the most significant exposure rather than addressing issues indiscriminately.

Threat intelligence also informs strategic planning. For example, insights into emerging attack techniques may influence technology adoption decisions or vendor selection. Intelligence related to supply chain threats may affect sourcing strategies and contract terms. In this way, cybersecurity becomes a factor in broader business strategy rather than an afterthought.

Another critical role of intelligence in decision making is scenario analysis. Predictive insights allow organizations to model potential future events and assess readiness. Leaders can evaluate how different threats might affect operations, finances, and reputation. This foresight supports contingency planning and strengthens resilience. Decisions are grounded in evidence rather than assumptions.

Communication is essential in this process. Threat intelligence must be presented in a form that non technical stakeholders can understand. Clear articulation of risk drivers, confidence levels, and potential outcomes bridges the gap between analysts and executives. When intelligence is communicated effectively, it builds trust and encourages informed engagement at leadership level.

Integrating threat intelligence into decision making also enhances accountability. When actions are based on documented intelligence, organizations can explain and justify choices to regulators, auditors, and stakeholders. This transparency supports governance and reinforces the credibility of cybersecurity programs.

Ultimately, the integration of threat intelligence into strategic decision making reflects organizational maturity. It signals a shift from viewing cybersecurity as a defensive function to recognizing it as a source of insight that shapes direction and performance.

Case Study: Using Threat Intelligence to Guide Strategic Investment in a Financial Services Firm

A regional financial services firm undergoing rapid digital expansion faced increasing exposure to cyber risk. The organization was investing in mobile platforms, automated lending systems, and data analytics capabilities to improve customer experience and operational efficiency. While these initiatives supported growth, they also introduced new dependencies and attack surfaces.

Initially, cybersecurity decisions were reactive. Investments were made in response to incidents or regulatory findings. Threat intelligence reports were reviewed by security teams but rarely discussed at executive level. As a result, leadership lacked a coherent view of cyber risk and struggled to prioritize investments.

The organization decided to reposition threat intelligence as a strategic input. Security and analytics teams collaborated to consolidate internal security data with external intelligence feeds. This information was analyzed to identify patterns relevant to the firm's specific operations, such as attacks targeting financial transaction workflows and customer authentication processes.

Insights were translated into business focused risk narratives. Rather than presenting lists of vulnerabilities, reports highlighted potential business impacts, including transaction fraud exposure, service disruption, and regulatory penalties. Predictive models estimated the likelihood of incidents based on current controls and projected growth.

These insights were presented to senior leadership during planning sessions. As a result, investment priorities shifted. Resources were allocated to strengthen authentication systems, enhance transaction monitoring, and improve vendor risk oversight. Some planned initiatives were redesigned to reduce exposure before launch.

The impact was measurable. Fraud attempts were detected earlier, reducing financial loss. Regulatory examinations became smoother due to improved risk documentation. Most importantly, leadership gained confidence in decision making. Cybersecurity was no longer viewed as a cost center, but as a source of intelligence that supported sustainable growth.

5.2 Operationalizing Predictive Security Across Enterprise Systems

While predictive security is often discussed as a modeling capability, its effectiveness depends on how well it is operationalized across enterprise systems. Predictive insight has limited value if it remains isolated within analytical tools or reports. To influence outcomes, predictions must be embedded into workflows, controls, and decision pathways where action can occur.

Operationalizing predictive security begins with integration. Predictive models must connect with operational systems such as identity management platforms, transaction engines, monitoring tools, and compliance systems. This integration ensures that when risk indicators emerge, responses can be triggered without delay. Predictive insights move from observation to intervention.

A key challenge in this process is translating probability into action. Predictive security models often generate risk scores or likelihood estimates rather than definitive alerts. Organizations must define thresholds and response strategies that align with their risk tolerance. These thresholds determine when automated controls are applied, when human review is required, and when activity is monitored without intervention.

Embedding predictive security into operations also requires alignment with business timing. Risk is not static throughout the day or business cycle. Certain periods such as financial close, peak transaction windows, or regulatory reporting deadlines carry higher sensitivity. Predictive systems that account for timing and operational context provide more relevant insight. This temporal awareness improves precision and reduces unnecessary disruption.

Another important aspect of operationalization is feedback. Predictive systems improve when outcomes are captured and analyzed. When interventions succeed or fail, that information should inform model refinement. This feedback loop strengthens accuracy over time and adapts predictions to evolving conditions. Without feedback, predictive security becomes stale and disconnected from reality.

Operationalizing predictive security also demands clear ownership. Multiple teams interact with predictive outputs, including security, operations, finance, and compliance. Roles must be defined to ensure accountability. Who approves automated actions? Who reviews model performance? Who updates thresholds when business conditions change? Clarity in these areas prevents confusion and ensures sustained effectiveness.

From a governance perspective, operationalized predictive security supports auditability. Actions taken based on predictions can be traced back to documented models, data sources, and decision rules. This traceability is essential in regulated environments where organizations must explain why certain actions were taken or why others were not.

Ultimately, predictive security becomes most powerful when it is treated as an operational capability rather than an analytical experiment. When embedded into enterprise systems, it enables earlier intervention, reduces uncertainty, and supports consistent risk management across complex environments.

Case Study: Embedding Predictive Security into Enterprise Risk Operations

A diversified enterprise operating across financial services, logistics, and digital platforms sought to improve its ability to anticipate cyber risk. The organization had invested in analytics and threat intelligence tools, but insights were largely confined to security teams. Operational leaders remained dependent on retrospective reports, limiting the organization's ability to act proactively.

To address this gap, the organization launched an initiative to operationalize predictive security across key systems. Historical security incidents, access logs, transaction data, and operational metrics were consolidated into a centralized analytics environment. Predictive models were developed to identify conditions associated with elevated risk, such as unusual access behavior combined with transaction anomalies during critical business periods.

Rather than generating alerts alone, predictive outputs were integrated into operational workflows. For example, when risk scores exceeded defined thresholds, additional authentication was required for sensitive transactions. In other cases, system changes were delayed pending review. These actions were aligned with business impact, ensuring proportional response.

The organization also established feedback mechanisms. Outcomes of predictive interventions were reviewed monthly. Models were refined based on false positives, missed signals, and changing business conditions. This iterative process improved accuracy and built trust among stakeholders.

Leadership engagement increased as predictive insights were incorporated into enterprise risk discussions. Rather than reacting to incidents, executives reviewed forward looking indicators during planning meetings. This shift supported better prioritization and more informed investment decisions.

The operational impact was significant. The organization experienced fewer high impact incidents and improved response times. Compliance teams reported greater confidence in risk controls due to documented predictive processes. Most importantly, predictive security became part of daily operations rather than an abstract concept.

Chapter 6

Risk and Compliance Management in Digitally Transformed Enterprises

Digital transformation has fundamentally altered how organizations perceive and manage risk. As business processes become increasingly automated, data driven, and interconnected, traditional approaches to risk and compliance management struggle to keep pace. What was once a periodic, document heavy exercise has evolved into a continuous, system embedded discipline that must operate alongside real time decision making.

In digitally transformed enterprises, risk is no longer confined to isolated functions. Technology, operations, finance, and compliance are tightly coupled. A change in one area can propagate across systems, affecting data integrity, regulatory posture, and financial performance simultaneously. Effective risk and compliance management therefore requires an integrated approach that reflects this interdependence.

One of the defining challenges of digital transformation is speed. Automated workflows execute decisions in milliseconds. Data pipelines update continuously. Cloud environments scale dynamically. In such conditions, delayed risk assessment can result in immediate exposure. Risk and compliance functions must evolve from retrospective review to proactive oversight. This shift demands tools and processes capable of operating at the same tempo as digital systems.

Data plays a central role in this evolution. Risk signals are embedded in transactional records, access logs, configuration changes, and analytics outputs. When these signals are aggregated and analyzed, they provide insight into emerging exposure. Data driven risk management leverages this information to identify trends, assess control effectiveness, and anticipate compliance gaps before they become violations.

Compliance requirements themselves are also changing. Regulators increasingly expect organizations to demonstrate not only adherence to rules, but also the effectiveness of controls. Evidence based compliance requires continuous monitoring, clear documentation, and traceable decision processes. Digitally transformed enterprises must show how controls operate in practice, not just how they are designed.

Another important consideration is regulatory complexity. Organizations often operate across multiple jurisdictions, each with distinct requirements. Digital platforms transcend geographic boundaries, making it challenging to apply consistent controls. Risk and compliance management must therefore balance standardization with flexibility. Centralized frameworks provide consistency, while localized adjustments address specific regulatory expectations.

Risk ownership is also evolving. In traditional models, risk and compliance were often centralized functions. In digital enterprises, ownership is distributed. Product teams, engineering groups, and operational units all influence risk through design and execution. Effective management requires clear accountability structures that define roles without creating bottlenecks. Collaboration becomes essential.

Technology enables this collaboration. Integrated risk platforms, analytics dashboards, and automated reporting tools provide shared visibility. When stakeholders access the same information, discussions become more productive. Decisions are based on evidence rather than assumptions. This transparency strengthens governance and supports faster response.

Digital transformation also introduces new risk categories. Cybersecurity risk intersects with financial risk, operational risk, and reputational risk. Data privacy, model bias, and system resilience become compliance considerations. Risk management frameworks must expand to address these dimensions holistically rather than treating them as separate issues.

Cost efficiency is another factor. Manual compliance processes are resource intensive and error prone. Automation reduces administrative burden and improves consistency. By embedding controls into systems, organizations reduce the need for after the fact remediation. This integration aligns risk management with performance objectives.

Leadership engagement is critical. Risk and compliance decisions influence strategic direction, investment, and innovation. Executives must understand how digital systems affect exposure and control. When leaders are informed, risk management becomes a strategic enabler rather than a constraint.

Continuous Compliance Monitoring in Automated Environments

One of the most significant shifts in risk and compliance management within digitally transformed enterprises is the move from periodic compliance checks to continuous compliance monitoring. Traditional compliance models were built around scheduled audits, manual reviews, and static documentation. While these approaches were sufficient in slower, less integrated environments, they are no longer adequate in systems that operate continuously and change rapidly.

Continuous compliance monitoring embeds regulatory and policy requirements directly into digital systems. Controls are enforced automatically, and compliance status is assessed in real time. This approach ensures that deviations are detected as they occur rather than weeks or months later. By reducing latency between noncompliance and detection, organizations can address issues before they escalate into violations or enforcement actions.

Automation plays a central role in this model. Configuration checks, access reviews, transaction monitoring, and policy validation can all be executed automatically. These checks generate evidence continuously, creating an auditable trail that reflects actual system behavior. This evidence based approach aligns closely with regulatory expectations, which increasingly emphasize demonstrable control effectiveness.

Continuous monitoring also improves consistency. Manual processes are susceptible to variation in interpretation and execution. Automated controls apply rules uniformly across environments, reducing the likelihood of oversight. This consistency is especially valuable in organizations operating across multiple platforms or jurisdictions, where maintaining alignment is challenging.

Another advantage of continuous compliance is adaptability. Regulatory requirements evolve, and organizations must respond quickly. When controls are embedded into systems, updates can be deployed centrally and enforced immediately. This agility reduces the risk of lag between regulatory change and compliance implementation.

From a governance perspective, continuous compliance monitoring enhances transparency. Stakeholders gain ongoing visibility into compliance posture, enabling informed oversight. Rather than relying on retrospective reports, leaders can assess risk exposure in near real time.

This visibility supports better decision making and reinforces accountability across teams.

However, continuous compliance also introduces new considerations. Organizations must ensure that automated controls reflect accurate interpretations of requirements. Oversight mechanisms are necessary to validate control logic and address exceptions. When implemented thoughtfully, continuous compliance transforms regulatory adherence from a reactive obligation into a proactive operational capability.

Analytics Driven Risk Quantification and Prioritization

In digitally transformed enterprises, the volume and variety of risk signals can be overwhelming. Effective risk management depends on the ability to quantify and prioritize exposure rather than treating all risks as equal. Analytics driven risk quantification provides the tools to evaluate likelihood, impact, and interdependencies in a structured manner.

Risk quantification begins with identifying relevant indicators. These may include system vulnerabilities, access anomalies, transaction irregularities, and operational performance metrics. Analytics aggregate these indicators and assess their relationships. By analyzing patterns over time, organizations gain insight into how risks emerge and escalate.

Quantification enables comparison. When risks are expressed in comparable terms, leaders can evaluate trade offs and allocate resources more effectively. For example, investments can be prioritized toward controls that reduce high impact risks rather than addressing low probability issues. This rational approach supports cost efficiency and strategic alignment.

Analytics also support scenario modeling. Organizations can simulate potential events and assess consequences under different conditions. This capability allows leaders to explore how changes in technology, process, or regulation might affect exposure. Scenario analysis enhances preparedness and informs strategic planning.

Another important benefit of analytics driven risk management is integration with financial performance. Risk metrics can be linked to financial outcomes such as revenue impact, remediation cost, and regulatory penalties. This integration makes risk discussions more concrete and relevant to business stakeholders. Cyber and compliance risks become part of enterprise risk management rather than isolated concerns.

Prioritization is essential in complex environments. Analytics highlight where controls are weakest, where dependencies create concentration risk, and where early intervention can prevent escalation. This focus enables targeted action rather than diffuse effort.

Governance considerations remain important. Models must be transparent and assumptions documented. Decision makers need confidence in the data and methods used. Clear communication of uncertainty supports informed judgment rather than false precision.

Analytics driven risk quantification shifts risk management from intuition to evidence. By grounding decisions in data, organizations improve consistency, accountability, and effectiveness. This analytical foundation prepares enterprises to address the financial implications of cybersecurity and compliance, which will be explored in the next chapter.

Chapter 7

Financial Analytics Models for Governance and Performance Tracking

In digitally transformed enterprises, financial performance is no longer shaped only by market conditions, pricing strategies, or cost structures. It is increasingly influenced by how well organizations manage digital risk, govern complex systems, and align operational activity with strategic intent. As cybersecurity, automation, and data driven processes become embedded in daily operations, financial analytics models emerge as essential tools for governance and performance tracking. They provide the structure through which leaders can understand value creation, exposure, and efficiency in environments where traditional accounting views are insufficient.

Financial analytics models extend beyond reporting revenue and expenses. They interpret how operational decisions affect financial outcomes over time. In digital enterprises, a single system misconfiguration, data integrity issue, or security lapse can have immediate financial consequences. These consequences may include fraud losses, regulatory penalties, service disruption, or erosion of customer trust. Financial analytics models capture these relationships, making them visible and measurable.

Governance depends on insight rather than volume of data. Boards and executive leaders are confronted with vast amounts of information, yet decision quality improves only when that information is structured and relevant. Financial analytics models translate technical and operational signals into indicators that support oversight. Metrics such as risk adjusted return, control effectiveness, cost of failure, and resilience related loss avoidance provide a clearer picture of organizational health than isolated financial statements.

One of the most important contributions of financial analytics is the ability to link investment decisions to outcomes. Cybersecurity, compliance, and digital infrastructure investments often compete for limited resources. Without analytics, these investments may be evaluated subjectively or treated as necessary overhead. Financial analytics models quantify their impact by measuring cost savings from prevented incidents, reductions in operational inefficiencies, and improvements in compliance efficiency. This evidence supports more disciplined capital allocation.

Cost transparency is another critical function. In complex organizations, costs associated with digital risk management are distributed across departments and budgets. Incident response, system maintenance, audit preparation, and remediation efforts all consume resources. Financial analytics models aggregate these costs and attribute them accurately. This visibility reveals hidden inefficiencies and supports optimization. Leaders gain a clearer understanding of where money is spent and why.

Performance tracking benefits from this transparency. Analytics models define key performance indicators that reflect both operational execution and risk posture. These indicators may include time to detect incidents, cost per compliance activity, financial impact of disruptions, and efficiency of automated controls. Tracking these metrics over time allows organizations to assess progress and identify trends. Improvement becomes measurable rather than assumed.

Integration across data domains is essential for meaningful financial analytics. Financial data alone cannot explain performance in digitally transformed environments. It must be connected with operational metrics, security events, and compliance indicators. When these data sources are analyzed together, organizations can see how technical conditions influence financial results. This integrated view supports balanced decision making and reduces the risk of unintended consequences.

Scenario analysis is another powerful application of financial analytics models. Digital enterprises face uncertainty related to cyber threats, regulatory change, and technological evolution. Scenario modeling allows organizations to explore potential futures and assess their financial implications. Leaders can evaluate how different risk events might affect cash flow, profitability, or capital requirements. This foresight supports preparedness and strengthens resilience.

Financial analytics also enhance accountability. When performance indicators are clearly defined and linked to organizational objectives, responsibility becomes explicit. Teams understand how their actions influence financial outcomes. This alignment encourages ownership and reinforces governance structures. Accountability is no longer abstract but grounded in measurable results.

Regulatory expectations increasingly require organizations to demonstrate understanding of financial risk related to technology and cybersecurity. Supervisory bodies expect evidence of stress testing, impact assessment, and control effectiveness. Financial analytics models provide the foundation for meeting these expectations. They support disclosures that reflect actual risk exposure and management capability.

Technology enables these analytics through data platforms, automation, and visualization tools. However, governance remains essential. Models must be developed using sound methodology, validated regularly, and documented clearly. Leaders must understand assumptions and limitations. Transparency builds trust and ensures responsible use of analytics in decision making.

Cultural adoption is equally important. Financial analytics models are effective only when they inform behavior. Leaders must engage with the insights produced and integrate them into governance discussions. When analytics become part of routine planning and review, organizations move toward evidence based management.

Importantly, financial analytics do not remove uncertainty. They provide structured insight rather than definitive answers. Effective governance requires interpreting analytics within context and combining them with professional judgment. Recognizing this balance prevents overreliance on models and supports sound decision making.

Linking Cyber and Operational Risk Metrics to Financial Performance

One of the most critical advancements in modern financial analytics is the ability to link cyber and operational risk metrics directly to financial performance indicators. In digitally transformed enterprises, risk events rarely remain isolated within technical systems. They influence revenue stability, cost structures, capital planning, and long term value creation. Financial analytics models provide the framework to make these relationships explicit and measurable.

Cyber incidents and operational disruptions often carry both direct and indirect financial consequences. Direct impacts may include fraud losses, remediation expenses, regulatory fines, or contractual penalties. Indirect impacts can be more difficult to quantify, such as customer attrition, reputational damage, delayed product launches, or reduced market confidence. Financial analytics models incorporate both dimensions to provide a fuller picture of exposure.

By mapping risk metrics to financial outcomes, organizations can evaluate the economic significance of control effectiveness. For example, metrics related to incident frequency, severity, and recovery time can be translated into expected loss estimates. These estimates allow leaders to compare the cost of preventive controls with the potential cost of inaction. This comparison supports rational investment decisions grounded in financial logic rather than fear or compliance pressure.

Linking risk and finance also improves prioritization. Not all risks warrant the same level of attention. Analytics highlight which vulnerabilities or process weaknesses pose the greatest threat to financial stability. This focus enables targeted mitigation efforts and avoids spreading resources too thinly. Financial relevance becomes a key criterion in risk evaluation.

Another benefit of this linkage is improved communication. Financially framed risk metrics are more accessible to non-technical stakeholders. Executives and board members can engage meaningfully with discussions about cyber and operational risk when impacts are expressed in familiar financial terms. This shared language strengthens governance and supports informed oversight.

Over time, organizations that integrate risk and financial analytics develop a more mature understanding of resilience. They move beyond viewing security and compliance as cost centers and begin to recognize their role in protecting value and supporting sustainable performance.

Performance Measurement Frameworks for Digital Governance

Effective governance in digitally transformed enterprises depends on the ability to measure performance across complex, interconnected systems. Financial analytics models support this need by enabling structured performance measurement frameworks that reflect both operational execution and strategic objectives. These frameworks provide clarity on how well the organization is managing resources, risk, and value creation.

Performance measurement frameworks define the indicators that matter most. In digital governance, these indicators extend beyond traditional financial ratios. They include measures related to system reliability, control efficiency, compliance responsiveness, and risk reduction. Financial analytics models integrate these indicators into cohesive views that support oversight and accountability.

A well designed framework balances leading and lagging indicators. Lagging indicators such as losses incurred or penalties paid reflect outcomes after events occur. Leading indicators such as control coverage, anomaly detection rates, or response effectiveness provide early signals of emerging issues. Financial analytics models incorporate both types, enabling proactive governance.

Consistency is another important consideration. Performance measurement frameworks must be applied uniformly across the organization to support comparison and trend analysis. Financial analytics models enforce this consistency by standardizing definitions, calculation methods, and reporting structures. This standardization reduces ambiguity and improves confidence in reported results.

Performance frameworks also support strategic alignment. Indicators should reflect organizational priorities and risk appetite. For example, an organization focused on growth may emphasize metrics related to scalability and control efficiency, while a highly regulated entity may prioritize compliance responsiveness and audit readiness. Financial analytics models allow these priorities to be reflected explicitly in performance tracking.

Accountability is reinforced when performance metrics are linked to roles and decision processes. Clear ownership of indicators encourages responsible behavior and continuous improvement. Financial analytics models support this linkage by providing traceable data and transparent calculations.

Importantly, performance measurement frameworks are not static. As digital strategies evolve, metrics must be reviewed and refined. Financial analytics models support this adaptability by enabling flexible analysis and scenario exploration. Governance remains dynamic rather than fixed.

Chapter 8

Data Driven Decision Making and Cost Efficiency in Modern Enterprises

In modern enterprises shaped by digital transformation, decision making has become one of the most critical determinants of performance, resilience, and long term competitiveness. Organizations now operate in environments where systems generate continuous streams of data, processes execute at machine speed, and market conditions shift rapidly. In this context, relying on intuition, precedent, or fragmented reporting is no longer sufficient. Data driven decision making has emerged as a foundational capability that enables organizations to navigate complexity while maintaining cost discipline and strategic clarity.

Data driven decision making refers to the systematic use of data, analytics, and evidence to inform choices at every level of the organization. It does not mean replacing human judgment with algorithms. Rather, it means grounding judgment in reliable insight. Decisions about investment, risk, operations, and growth are increasingly shaped by patterns identified in data rather than assumptions or anecdotal experience. This shift fundamentally changes how organizations manage cost efficiency.

Cost inefficiency often thrives in opacity. When leaders lack visibility into how resources are consumed, inefficiencies persist unnoticed. Digital enterprises are particularly vulnerable to this problem because costs are embedded across platforms, subscriptions, automation tools, security controls, and compliance processes. Individually, these costs may appear reasonable. Collectively, they can erode margins and constrain innovation. Data driven analysis brings these dispersed costs into focus.

One of the primary benefits of data driven decision making is the ability to identify true cost drivers. Rather than relying on aggregate budgets or high level expense categories, analytics reveal which processes, systems, or behaviors generate disproportionate cost. For example, repeated manual interventions in automated workflows, excessive exception handling, or redundant controls may signal deeper inefficiencies. When these patterns are identified, organizations can address root causes rather than applying superficial cost reductions.

Data driven approaches also improve the accuracy of trade off analysis. Many decisions involve balancing cost against risk, speed, or quality. Without data, these trade-offs are often resolved subjectively. Analytics quantify impact. Leaders can evaluate whether additional controls reduce risk sufficiently to justify their cost, or whether process redesign delivers better efficiency without compromising governance. This analytical clarity supports disciplined decision making.

Another important dimension is timing. Costs often escalate when issues are detected late. Delayed identification of inefficiencies, control failures, or performance degradation leads to reactive spending on remediation. Data driven monitoring enables earlier intervention. By detecting anomalies and trends in near real time, organizations can correct course before costs compound. Prevention becomes more economical than correction.

Data driven decision making also supports scalability. As organizations grow, manual oversight becomes impractical. Decisions must be delegated and often automated. Analytics provide the framework for consistent decision logic across scale. When rules and thresholds are informed by data, automated decisions align more closely with organizational objectives. This alignment reduces waste and supports predictable performance.

Consistency is a recurring theme. In organizations where decisions vary widely based on individual discretion, cost efficiency suffers. Data driven frameworks standardize evaluation criteria. Teams operate from shared metrics and definitions. This consistency reduces duplication, prevents conflicting actions, and improves coordination. Over time, standardized decision making contributes to operational maturity.

Transparency is another critical benefit. When decisions are supported by data, they can be explained clearly. Stakeholders understand why resources were allocated in certain ways and how outcomes are measured. This transparency strengthens governance and builds trust. It also supports accountability. When outcomes diverge from expectations, data provides a basis for learning rather than blame.

Data driven decision making also reshapes how organizations approach budgeting and planning. Traditional budgeting often relies on historical spend adjusted incrementally. Analytics enable more dynamic planning. Forecasts can incorporate current performance trends, risk indicators, and scenario analysis. Budgets become living instruments rather than static constraints. This flexibility supports cost efficiency by aligning spend with evolving priorities.

Importantly, data driven decision making requires cultural change. Organizations must value evidence over hierarchy and inquiry over certainty. Leaders must be willing to challenge assumptions and revise decisions based on new information. This cultural shift is often more difficult than deploying analytics tools. Without it, data remains underutilized.

Governance plays a crucial role in ensuring that data driven decisions remain aligned with organizational values. Analytics can highlight opportunities for cost reduction that conflict with ethical, regulatory, or strategic considerations. Oversight frameworks ensure that efficiency gains do not undermine trust, compliance, or long term resilience. Data informs decisions, but governance guides them.

Cost efficiency achieved through data driven decision making is not synonymous with austerity. It is about optimizing value. Organizations that understand their cost structures deeply can invest confidently in areas that drive growth and resilience. Efficiency becomes a source of strategic advantage rather than a defensive response to pressure.

Another important aspect is learning. Data driven decision making creates feedback loops. Outcomes are measured, insights refined, and decisions improved over time. This continuous learning supports adaptation in changing environments. Organizations become better decision makers as they accumulate evidence and experience.

Data quality remains foundational. Poor data leads to poor decisions. Enterprises must invest in data governance practices that ensure accuracy, completeness, and relevance. This investment underpins all analytical efforts. Without reliable data, even the most sophisticated models fail to deliver value.

In digitally transformed enterprises, decision making increasingly occurs within systems. Automated approvals, dynamic pricing, and risk based controls execute decisions continuously. Human oversight remains essential to set boundaries, review outcomes, and intervene when necessary. Data driven governance ensures that automation serves organizational objectives rather than undermining them.

Embedding Analytics into Executive and Operational Decision Structures

A critical yet often underdeveloped aspect of data driven decision making is how analytics are embedded into the actual structures where decisions occur. Many organizations invest heavily in dashboards, reports, and analytical tools, yet fail to integrate these insights into executive forums, operational reviews, and daily management routines. As a result, analytics exist in parallel to decision making rather than shaping it.

Embedding analytics into decision structures requires intentional design. Executive committees, risk councils, and operational review meetings must be structured around data rather than presentations alone. When analytics become the starting point for discussion, conversations shift from opinion based debate to evidence informed evaluation. Decisions are framed around what the data indicates, what assumptions underlie the analysis, and what actions are justified.

This embedding also requires alignment between analytical outputs and decision horizons. Strategic decisions require aggregated, forward looking insight. Operational decisions require granular, near real time data. When analytics are mismatched to decision context, they are ignored or misused. Effective embedding ensures that the right level of insight reaches the right decision makers at the right time.

Another important factor is ownership. Analytics must have clear custodians who are responsible for data quality, interpretation, and communication. Without ownership, insights lose credibility. Decision makers need confidence that analytics reflect reality and are maintained consistently. This trust encourages reliance on data rather than intuition.

Embedding analytics also supports cost discipline. When cost drivers and efficiency indicators are reviewed regularly within decision forums, inefficiencies are addressed systematically. Cost management becomes proactive rather than reactive. Leaders recognize patterns early and intervene before waste accumulates.

Cultural reinforcement is equally important. Organizations must reward evidence based decisions and discourage reliance on unsupported assertions. Over time, this culture shift normalizes data driven reasoning. Decisions are challenged constructively, and learning becomes continuous.

Importantly, embedding analytics does not mean rigid adherence to numbers. Context, judgment, and ethical considerations remain essential. Analytics inform decisions, but leaders retain responsibility for interpreting implications and managing trade offs. When analytics and judgment work together, decision quality improves significantly.

Case Study: Improving Cost Discipline Through Analytics Embedded in Executive Governance

A technology enabled services organization experienced persistent cost overruns despite strong revenue growth. Leadership relied on periodic financial reports and departmental summaries to guide decisions. While these reports provided high level visibility, they lacked insight into operational drivers of cost inefficiency.

The organization initiated a program to embed analytics directly into executive governance structures. Financial, operational, and risk data were integrated into a unified analytics platform. Key indicators related to cost efficiency, system utilization, and process performance were identified. These indicators were reviewed consistently during executive meetings rather than as supplementary material.

Analytics revealed that cost overruns were driven by a small number of recurring issues, including duplicated processes across teams, excessive manual intervention in automated workflows, and inconsistent vendor utilization. These insights were not apparent in traditional reports, which aggregated costs at too high a level.

Armed with this evidence, leadership implemented targeted interventions. Processes were redesigned to reduce duplication. Automation thresholds were adjusted to minimize manual overrides. Vendor contracts were renegotiated based on usage data. Because decisions were grounded in analytics, interventions were focused and measurable.

Within months, cost variability decreased and forecasting accuracy improved. Executives reported greater confidence in decision making because discussions were anchored in shared evidence. Cost discipline became embedded in governance rather than enforced through isolated cost cutting initiatives.

Using Predictive Analytics to Control Cost Escalation and Resource Drift

Cost inefficiency in modern enterprises rarely appears suddenly. It develops gradually through small deviations, delayed decisions, and resource drift across systems and teams. Predictive analytics plays a crucial role in addressing this challenge by identifying early indicators of cost escalation before they translate into material financial impact. Rather than responding after budgets are exceeded, organizations can intervene while corrective action remains low cost and minimally disruptive.

Predictive analytics uses historical patterns, behavioral trends, and operational signals to forecast future outcomes. In the context of cost management, this means identifying combinations of activity that historically lead to overspending, inefficiency, or waste. These indicators may include rising exception rates, increasing manual intervention in automated processes, abnormal system utilization, or repeated short term fixes that mask structural issues.

One of the key advantages of predictive analytics is its ability to detect compound effects. Cost escalation often results from multiple small factors interacting over time. Predictive models capture these interactions by analyzing relationships across data sets rather than evaluating metrics in isolation. This holistic view enables earlier and more accurate identification of risk.

Predictive analytics also supports smarter resource allocation. By forecasting demand and utilization trends, organizations can adjust staffing, infrastructure capacity, and vendor engagement proactively. This foresight reduces both overprovisioning and underinvestment. Resources are aligned with actual needs rather than reactive assumptions.

Another important dimension is prioritization. Not all cost risks require immediate action. Predictive models estimate likelihood and potential impact, allowing leaders to focus attention where intervention will deliver the greatest benefit. This targeted approach avoids unnecessary disruption and supports disciplined cost management.

Integration with governance processes is essential. Predictive insights must feed into planning cycles, budget reviews, and operational oversight forums. When predictions are treated as decision inputs rather than informational outputs, they influence behavior. Cost management becomes forward looking rather than retrospective.

Transparency also matters. Decision makers need to understand how predictions are generated and what assumptions they reflect. Clear communication builds trust and encourages appropriate use. Predictive analytics should inform judgment, not replace it.

By enabling early intervention and informed prioritization, predictive analytics transforms cost management into a proactive discipline. Organizations gain the ability to steer performance deliberately rather than correcting course after inefficiencies have already taken hold.

Case Study: Preventing Cost Drift in a Digitally Scaling Enterprise

A rapidly growing digital services company faced increasing difficulty controlling operational costs as it expanded into new markets. While revenue growth remained strong, margins fluctuated unpredictably. Traditional financial reporting revealed overspending only after it had already occurred, limiting leadership's ability to respond effectively.

To address this challenge, the organization implemented predictive analytics focused on cost behavior. Historical data from operations, finance, and technology platforms was analyzed to identify patterns associated with cost escalation. These patterns included increases in system exceptions, delays in process completion, and spikes in manual intervention during peak periods.

Predictive models were developed to flag early warning signals. When thresholds were exceeded, alerts were generated for operational and financial leaders. These alerts did not mandate action, but prompted review and discussion. Leaders could examine underlying drivers and determine appropriate responses.

As predictive insights were integrated into planning and review cycles, behavior changed. Teams addressed issues earlier, adjusting workflows and resource allocation before costs accumulated. Vendor usage was optimized based on forecasted demand rather than historical averages. Automation settings were refined to reduce unnecessary manual work.

Over time, cost variability decreased and forecasting accuracy improved. Leaders gained confidence in their ability to manage growth without sacrificing efficiency. Predictive analytics shifted the organization from reactive cost control to proactive performance management.

Chapter 9

Real World Applications of Cybersecurity and Data Innovation in Business Transformation

Business transformation is rarely achieved through technology alone. It occurs when organizations apply technology deliberately to reshape how value is created, protected, and sustained. Cybersecurity and data innovation play a central role in this transformation by enabling trust, insight, and operational confidence in environments defined by speed and complexity. This chapter examines how these capabilities are applied in real world organizational contexts to drive meaningful change.

At the core of transformation is alignment. Organizations that succeed do not treat cybersecurity and data analytics as isolated functions. Instead, they integrate them into business strategy, operations, and governance. Security controls are designed to support growth rather than restrict it. Data analytics informs decisions at every level, from daily operations to long term planning. This alignment allows transformation initiatives to scale without introducing unacceptable risk.

One of the most visible applications of cybersecurity in business transformation is the enablement of digital platforms. Online services, mobile applications, and automated customer interactions depend on secure access, data integrity, and availability. Without robust security, these platforms cannot earn trust. Cybersecurity provides the foundation that allows organizations to expand digital offerings confidently, knowing that customer data and transactions are protected.

Data innovation complements this foundation by turning operational activity into insight. As organizations digitize processes, they generate data that reveals how systems perform and where value is created or lost. Analytics identify bottlenecks, inefficiencies, and emerging opportunities. When combined with secure data handling practices, this insight supports transformation that is both innovative and responsible.

Another important application is in operational optimization. Many organizations use analytics to redesign workflows, reduce manual effort, and improve responsiveness. Cybersecurity ensures that these optimizations do not introduce new vulnerabilities. Controls are embedded into redesigned processes, maintaining oversight as automation increases. The result is improved efficiency without sacrificing control.

Financial transformation also benefits from the integration of cybersecurity and data analytics. Automated financial reporting, real time performance tracking, and predictive forecasting depend on accurate and secure data. Cybersecurity protects the integrity of financial information, while analytics provide visibility into trends and risks. Together, they support more informed financial management and stronger governance.

In regulated industries, cybersecurity and data innovation enable compliance by design. Rather than retrofitting controls to meet regulatory requirements, organizations embed compliance into systems and processes. Analytics monitor adherence continuously, and security controls enforce policy automatically. This approach reduces compliance burden and improves audit readiness, supporting transformation without regulatory friction.

Customer experience is another area where these capabilities intersect. Personalized services, rapid response, and seamless interactions depend on data driven insight. At the same time, customers expect privacy and protection. Cybersecurity safeguards customer data, while analytics tailor experiences responsibly. Organizations that balance these priorities build trust and loyalty.

Transformation also extends to organizational culture. When leaders use data to guide decisions and treat cybersecurity as a shared responsibility, behavior changes. Teams become more disciplined, collaborative, and accountable. Data literacy improves, and security awareness becomes part of daily practice. This cultural shift reinforces transformation efforts and sustains progress.

Importantly, real world applications reveal that transformation is iterative. Organizations rarely achieve perfection on the first attempt. They learn through experimentation, measurement, and adjustment. Cybersecurity and data innovation support this learning by providing feedback and control. Failures are detected early, and insights guide refinement.

These applications demonstrate that cybersecurity and data innovation are not abstract concepts. They are practical tools that reshape how organizations operate, compete, and grow. When applied thoughtfully, they enable transformation that is resilient, efficient, and aligned with strategic objectives.

Transforming Enterprise Trust Through Secure Data Ecosystems

One of the most significant outcomes of applying cybersecurity and data innovation in real world business environments is the transformation of trust. Trust is no longer based solely on brand reputation or contractual assurance. In digital enterprises, trust is built through the consistent protection, accuracy, and responsible use of data. Secure data ecosystems form the backbone of this trust.

A secure data ecosystem is one in which data is protected across its entire lifecycle, from creation and storage to processing, sharing, and archival. Cybersecurity ensures that access is controlled, usage is monitored, and integrity is preserved. Data innovation adds the capability to analyze and validate data continuously. Together, these elements create confidence among stakeholders that information can be relied upon.

Enterprise trust extends beyond customers. Investors, regulators, partners, and employees all depend on the reliability of digital systems. When cybersecurity controls are embedded into data workflows, organizations reduce uncertainty and demonstrate operational maturity. This trust enables broader collaboration, smoother partnerships, and greater willingness to adopt new digital services.

Trust also influences strategic flexibility. Organizations with secure data ecosystems can move faster because they spend less time managing risk reactively. Decisions are supported by reliable information, and transformation initiatives face fewer internal objections related to uncertainty or exposure. Cybersecurity and data innovation therefore function as enablers of agility rather than constraints.

Another important aspect is transparency. Secure data ecosystems support traceability and auditability. Stakeholders can understand how data is used, how decisions are made, and how controls are enforced. This transparency strengthens accountability and reinforces trust over time.

By transforming trust from an abstract value into a measurable capability, organizations create a competitive advantage. Secure and well governed data ecosystems support sustainable transformation and long term value creation.

Scaling Digital Transformation Without Compounding Risk

Scaling transformation is one of the most difficult challenges organizations face. Early successes often give way to complexity as systems expand, integrations multiply, and automation increases. Without disciplined cybersecurity and data innovation, scaling amplifies risk rather than value. Effective application of these capabilities enables organizations to grow while maintaining control.

Cybersecurity provides the structure required to manage scale. Standardized controls, automated enforcement, and consistent monitoring reduce variability across environments. As new systems and services are introduced, they inherit baseline protections. This consistency prevents the accumulation of unmanaged risk that often accompanies rapid growth.

Data innovation supports scale by maintaining insight as complexity increases. Analytics aggregate signals across systems, revealing patterns that would otherwise be obscured. Leaders can assess performance, risk, and efficiency across the enterprise rather than relying on fragmented views. This visibility is essential for governing large, distributed operations.

Scaling without compounding risk also requires disciplined integration. New technologies, vendors, and partners must align with existing security and data standards. Cybersecurity frameworks and data governance policies provide criteria for evaluation and onboarding. This discipline ensures that growth does not undermine foundational controls.

Cost efficiency is another consideration. Scaling often increases cost if inefficiencies are replicated. Data driven insight identifies where processes can be optimized and where investment delivers diminishing returns. Cybersecurity automation reduces the marginal cost of protection as scale increases. Together, these capabilities support sustainable growth.

Ultimately, scaling transformation successfully requires balance. Organizations must pursue innovation while maintaining oversight.

Cybersecurity and data innovation provide the mechanisms to achieve this balance. They enable expansion that is resilient, controlled, and aligned with strategic intent.

Chapter 10

Sustaining Cybersecurity and Data Innovation for the Future of Business

Business transformation does not end with implementation. It is sustained through discipline, adaptation, and continuous learning. As organizations become more digital, more data driven, and more interconnected, cybersecurity and data innovation must evolve from project based initiatives into enduring organizational capabilities.

The defining characteristic of the future business environment is change. Technologies evolve rapidly, regulatory expectations shift, and threat actors adapt continuously. In this context, static approaches to cybersecurity and analytics are insufficient. Organizations must build systems and cultures that anticipate change rather than react to it. Sustainability depends on flexibility grounded in strong foundations.

When security is treated as a technical afterthought, it lags behind transformation efforts and introduces friction. When it is integrated into strategy, it enables confidence and speed. Sustaining this integration requires ongoing dialogue between technical leaders and business decision makers. Cybersecurity priorities must be revisited regularly as business models evolve.

Data innovation follows a similar trajectory. Analytics capabilities must mature alongside organizational needs. Early successes in reporting and optimization should lead to more advanced applications such as predictive insight and automated decision support. However, sophistication must be matched with governance. As models influence more decisions, transparency, accountability, and ethical considerations become increasingly important. Sustainable innovation balances ambition with responsibility.

Talent and culture play a central role in sustaining capability. Technology alone does not create resilience. Organizations must invest in people who understand both the technical and business dimensions of cybersecurity and analytics. Cross functional collaboration should be encouraged, and learning should be continuous. When teams share a common understanding of risk, data, and value, coordination improves and silos diminish.

Leadership commitment is essential. Executives and boards set the tone for how seriously cybersecurity and data innovation are treated. Sustained progress requires visible support, clear accountability, and willingness to invest. Leaders must engage with analytics and risk information actively, using it to inform decisions rather than delegating responsibility entirely. This engagement reinforces the strategic importance of these capabilities.

Governance frameworks must also evolve. As automation and artificial intelligence become more embedded, oversight mechanisms must ensure alignment with organizational values and regulatory expectations. Policies should be reviewed regularly, and controls tested continuously. Governance is not a constraint on innovation. It is the structure that allows innovation to scale safely.

Another key consideration is ecosystem engagement. Few organizations operate in isolation. Partners, vendors, and platforms form complex networks of dependency. Sustaining cybersecurity and data innovation requires extending standards and expectations across these networks. Collaboration and information sharing enhance collective resilience. Organizations that engage proactively with their ecosystems are better positioned to manage shared risk.

Measurement remains critical. What gets measured gets managed. Performance indicators related to security effectiveness, decision quality, cost efficiency, and resilience provide feedback on progress. These metrics should evolve as capabilities mature. Continuous measurement supports learning and adjustment, preventing stagnation.

Looking ahead, emerging technologies will introduce new opportunities and risks. Artificial intelligence will become more autonomous. Data volumes will grow. Regulatory scrutiny will increase. Organizations that have embedded cybersecurity and data innovation into their core operations will adapt more easily. Those that have not will struggle to keep pace.

Ultimately, sustaining transformation is about mindset. Cybersecurity and data innovation should be viewed not as destinations, but as ongoing journeys. They require curiosity, vigilance, and commitment. Organizations that embrace this mindset will be better equipped to protect value, drive performance, and navigate uncertainty.

Building Adaptive Cybersecurity and Data Capabilities Over Time

Sustaining cybersecurity and data innovation requires organizations to move beyond static maturity models and embrace adaptability as a core principle. Capabilities that are effective today may become insufficient tomorrow as technologies, threats, and business models evolve. Adaptive capability building ensures that systems, processes, and skills evolve in tandem with external and internal change.

Adaptability begins with architectural flexibility. Systems should be designed to accommodate change without extensive rework. Modular architectures, standardized interfaces, and configurable controls allow organizations to update defenses and analytics models efficiently. This flexibility reduces the cost and disruption associated with change and supports continuous improvement.

Processes must also adapt. Risk assessments, model validation, and governance reviews should be iterative rather than episodic. Feedback from incidents, audits, and performance metrics informs refinement. Organizations that institutionalize learning are better equipped to anticipate emerging challenges and adjust proactively.

Skill development is another critical factor. As cybersecurity and analytics tools become more sophisticated, the skills required to manage them evolve. Continuous training, cross functional exposure, and knowledge sharing help maintain capability relevance. Organizations that invest in people alongside technology sustain advantage over time.

Adaptability also requires openness to experimentation. Controlled pilots, sandbox environments, and incremental deployment allow organizations to test new approaches without excessive risk. Insights gained through experimentation inform broader adoption. This disciplined innovation supports progress while maintaining control.

By treating cybersecurity and data innovation as evolving capabilities rather than fixed solutions, organizations create resilience. They remain responsive to change and capable of sustaining transformation in uncertain environments.

Preparing for Ethical, Regulatory, and Societal Expectations

As cybersecurity and data innovation become central to business operations, organizations face growing ethical, regulatory, and societal expectations. Stakeholders increasingly demand not only effectiveness, but responsibility. Sustaining transformation therefore requires deliberate attention to how technology is used and governed.

Ethical considerations extend beyond compliance. Decisions influenced by data and automation can affect individuals, communities, and markets. Organizations must consider fairness, transparency, and accountability in system design and operation. Ethical frameworks guide decision making and prevent unintended harm.

Regulatory expectations are also evolving. Authorities expect organizations to demonstrate control over automated systems, explain decision logic, and manage risk proactively. Sustained capability requires staying ahead of regulatory change rather than reacting to enforcement. Continuous monitoring, documentation, and engagement with regulators support this readiness.

Societal trust is another dimension. Customers and partners increasingly evaluate organizations based on how they handle data and protect digital environments. Trust is built through consistent behavior, clear communication, and demonstrated responsibility. Cybersecurity and data innovation practices shape reputation as much as performance.

Preparing for these expectations requires integration. Ethics, compliance, and security should not operate in silos. Governance frameworks must align principles across domains. Leadership must articulate values clearly and reinforce them through policy and practice.

By addressing ethical, regulatory, and societal considerations proactively, organizations strengthen legitimacy and sustainability. Cybersecurity and data innovation become not only tools for performance, but foundations for responsible leadership in a digital world.

www.ingramcontent.com/pod-product-compliance
Lightning Source LLC
Chambersburg PA
CBHW051352240926
51852CB00001B/4
9783383456725